The Rose

Delores L. Kendrick

The Rose

ISBN 978-0-9961444-6-9

Published by Marion Street Publishing

Designed by Lynette Winters, Jewell Evans

Cover Photo: Yuen Li

For Edwin and Josie

Acknowledgments

First, I want to thank the Lord for loving me and giving me the courage to write my story. Without Him I would not be here today. He is my strength, my joy, the very breath I breathe. He is my inspiration.

To my children and granddaughter, who have always been a great support and encouragement to me. You allowed me to sacrifice time away from you so that I could obey the Lord and write this book. You released me to hold nothing back, but to tell my story. For this, I will be forever grateful.

To my church, Tabernacle of Praise, who have been supportive and loyal, I thank you.

With great gratitude, I thank and acknowledge Lynette Winters, who first approached me to write, and gave me her full financial support in editing, and guiding me through to the completion of this book.

Thank you Doctor Marilyn Nilsson for assisting with the editing.

Thank you, Nora Lynn, who was my best friend during those difficult years. Thank you for allowing me to share details of our life while married to best friends.

Special thanks to Pastors Robert and Beverly Evans for their love, prayers, and faithful support throughout the years. Pastor Evans who was a spiritual father to my girls, is now one of the great cloud of witnesses in glory.

Finally, to those who shall read *The Rose*: Be strong and courageous. Do not be frightened, and do not be dismayed, for the Lord your God is with you wherever you go.

Table of Contents

Edwin & Josie

I thank my God in my remembrance of you.

I grew up in Seattle, Washington where I attended elementary school through high school. My parents left Shreveport, Louisiana for more job opportunities for their family. I had awesome parents! My dad was a hardworking man and my mother was a stay-at-home mom. I remember the bond that we had as children growing up. My dad was a carefree, fun-loving easy-going dad, with a million-dollar smile. My mother said when he proposed to her, he asked her if she was willing to be a stay-at-home mom; he wanted his children to always have her in the home for them.

My father was a hardworking man who adored his children and treated my mother like a queen. There was very little she wanted that he did not in some way get it for her. I remember after working long hours, he would come in late at night and he would bake gingerbread. My dad was an amazing baker. I would wake up with those large but gentle hands shaking me gently to hot gingerbread and a cold glass of milk. Yes, I am sure he was tired, but those were memories I will always cherish. He loved his children and never failed to express it in many loving ways.

When I was a little girl, I would cook on my little stove...*Big Chief* it was called. My mother would give me some of the batter, and I would pour it into my little pound cake pan and put it into my little chief oven. She would start cooking the vegetables, and just before they were finished, she would give them to me to finish cooking on my little stove. The stove didn't produce a lot of heat, so this way I felt as though I was cooking the meal for my father. I had beautiful, yet very small, China dishes that my parents' friend gave me. He was a seaman and traveled often. He got me a set of little China dishes for Christmas. This is what I served my father in when he would come home from work before we sat for dinner. He would take the little teacup in those big hands and sip the tea, as we sat on the floor and ate the food I prepared for him.

He could have picked up the roast and ate it in one bite since it was so small. The little muffins in my muffin pan were so tiny, but he would take his time and try to cut and butter them. And of course, we had to have dessert.

I thought I had the best dad in the world. He was my hero! When I look back on those precious memories, I can't help but lift my hands in praise to God for giving me, such wonderful parents. I remember so many wonderful memories. It would be impossible to tell them all, for this book would not be able to contain them.

My mom was more structured and trained us to be people of character and integrity. She loved serving and she taught us to work hard and prepared us to face the world.

She was an expert cook and her table was always set in excellence. On Sundays, we had four-course meals. We would join hands and my dad would pray, and then we would share in fellowship.

Mother taught me to cook, sew, clean, and whatever it took to make me a woman of excellence. I was a skinny little girl, growing faster than I wanted to, and very self-conscious of my height. My feet were long and narrow. I felt as if they were the longest feet in the world. I would slump when I stood because I felt that made me look shorter. Mother, aware of my dilemma, would encourage me, and tell me one day I would be happy over my height. She would have me practice walking with a book on my head, tucking my tummy in, and standing straight with my shoulders back. I remember she showed me a picture of *Jane Russell* because I believe she was 5'7" and was very beautiful. Well, I knew I would never be a *Jane Russell*, but oh well, if a movie star could be tall, surely, I could live through it.

I was raised with three brothers who were older than me. I was the baby of the family and the only girl. It was interesting growing up because I was a tomboy following my brothers and being a constant pest. On the other hand, my mother instilled in me that I was a young girl who would grow up to be a young lady one day, so I would have to start acting like one. Even though I was raised with three boys, my mother was determined I would know my identity as a young lady, and I would have the grace, character, and dignity to become all God had purposed for my life. I will forever thank God for choosing my parents.

I have learned to appreciate this quality which she displayed throughout my childhood. I am no way implying that she had all the answers, but the wisdom she had gained from observing others, she applied in our home… as I did later in my life. My mother did not finish high school, but she was blessed to be around those who mentored and instilled in her certain life virtues which made her a great example to me as well as others.

No, my parents were not perfect; but they were perfect for me.

The Day Heaven Opened

Drip down, O heavens, from above, and let the clouds pour down righteousness; Let the earth open up and salvation bear fruit, And righteousness spring up with it. I, the LORD, have created it

Isaiah 45:8

My parents were God-fearing people and were faithful in their convictions as Christians. They took us to church each Sunday and we also attended church on Sunday evening. I would often hear my father playing the piano in the front room (that's what we called it) and my mother singing. She had a beautiful voice and he had a gift for playing the piano. My mother was a dedicated prayer warrior and she would pray and sing throughout the house all the time. My dad would challenge me to memorize chapters in the Bible, which became a hobby of mine.

I would attend an all-black Baptist church on Sunday morning and throughout the week I attended an all-white Assemblies of God Church.

One afternoon while playing house out on our front lawn with my best friend Judy, I experienced something that was the beginning of a new day for me. Our lawn was well-manicured, with perfectly trimmed hedges surrounding the house. We placed the little table on the lawn. We gathered the little berries from the trees, pretending this was our meal. We made mud pies. This may seem strange to many today, but this is how we used to play house in my day as a nine-year-old. You see, we still played with dolls and we still cut paper dolls. As we finished cooking our play meal, we set the table with our plastic plates and forks, and I looked at Judy and said, "Ok, now we are ready for our dinner so we must bless the food." She did not have a clue what I was talking about, (what was she doing?) so I said, "We must say grace." So, Judy said, "Oh, ok, grace." I said, "No, Judy, we must thank God for our food we are going to eat." So, I told her to let's hold hands, bow our heads and close our eyes.

It was a beautiful summer day in Seattle...there was not a cloud in the sky. The sky was blue. I will never forget the beauty of the heavens that day. For some reason, I lifted my head rather than bowing it, as we did at home around the table when my father prayed the blessing on the food. I began to pray.

"Lord bless this food we are about to receive...", and that is as far as I got. Suddenly, the heavens opened, and I felt something I had never felt before. It seemed as though Heaven opened up and came down upon me. I was embraced in a presence I never felt before. I jumped up and knocked the table over and started running to the house. I was banging on the door. My mother came and opened the door and took one look at me and said, "Oh Lord my child is saved!" I fell into my mother's arms and we cried together. In a moment, my heart had changed and this little nine-year-old experienced salvation. My parents and I had some beautiful times together as they shared and explained to me the Gospel of Jesus Christ. I told my pastor that I had accepted Christ into my heart, and I wanted to be baptized.

I was later baptized in Lake Washington on a Sunday morning. What a day that was...I will never forget it! I was led out onto the lake where they sang *Take Me to the Water to Be*

Baptized...That was an old song. I can almost hear the gospel choir singing it now. All I remember was, that I was walking through the little ripples in the water toward the elders who were waiting to baptize me. I went down in the water and then the next thing I knew, I was on the shore crying and praising God. Heaven smiled on me that Sunday afternoon.

You would ask, "What happened to Judy?" I don't know. I guess she ran the other way for fear of what had taken place at the dinner table.

My life had changed drastically. I would have dreams and the Lord began to speak to me and teach me how to pray.

I went to a camp meeting for three days at Lake Wilderness when I was eleven years old, and I received the Baptism in the Holy Spirit with the evidence of speaking in other tongues. I was so drunk in the spirit that I sang all the way home in the car. The Pastor tried to calm me down, but he gave up. He was concerned about what my mother would think, as she had not yet experienced the baptism.

I remember getting out of the car and the pastor and his wife leading me up the steps to the door. My mother came to the door and I just fell in her arms, I was so happy. I was experiencing what the apostle's experienced at Pentecost in the book of Acts 2:4 "And they were all filled with the Holy Ghost, and began to speak with other tongues, as the Spirit gave them utterance."

They explained to my mother what had happened to me. I remember her words, "Is this going to make her keep her room clean now?"

Mother did not understand what I had just experienced, but she recognized the presence of God. She was a strong Christian, so she never questioned or had any doubt that my experience was real.

Six years later, my mother was filled with the Holy Spirit while talking on the phone; yes, with the same pastor that prayed me through. I remember that afternoon coming down the stairs, from my bedroom, headed to the kitchen. I heard my mother on the phone with the pastor. She was speaking louder than usual, her words were: "Listen, Pastor, if God wanted me to speak in tongues, He would do it because I believe in every book, every chapter, and every line." All of a sudden I heard the most beautiful language pouring out of my mother's mouth. It was the heavenly language of the Spirit. She was looking at the phone as though she did not know what in the world had happened to her. She rejoiced all day, shouting and praising God for her new experience. One year after that, my father also was filled with the Holy Spirit. Reverend Norman Hutchcroft was one of the most precious men of God I have ever known. It was through his sharing the Gospel in its entirety that my family received Christ into their lives.

The Great Awakening

Can two walk together, except they be agreed?

Amos 3:3

I was not one to date a lot in high school. As a matter of fact, I only dated one person, who later became my husband and the father of my two girls.

I had drifted away from my faith over the years. I was not spiritually where I should have been with God. Yes, I went to church, but the passion I once had was not there. My relationship had been diluted with teen life. I became lazy in my pursuit for what the divine purpose of my life really was. I was caught up with the activities of the teenager's life. I had let the thief come in and steal that intimacy, that desire, that precious love that had lit the fire to my intimacy with the Lord. The enemy of your flesh is so subtle, so smooth, you will realize that the connection has been broken, and you can't even figure out how. When did it happen? You can't name the date, the time or the place. You were just once alive in Him; now, you are only existing.

I remember on my wedding day, as I was preparing to walk down the aisle, holding my father's arm, he stopped and looked at me with those gentle loving gray eyes. He said, "Honey are you sure this is what you want?" I nodded with uncertainty because I feared if I would speak, I probably would have said "*no*" and everyone would have seen a preview of '*Runaway Bride*' featuring Delores, rather than Julia Roberts. I convinced myself it was just the doubt that comes before a wedding, which was normal. Have you ever come to a place in your life where you knew in the back of your mind you were hoping you were not making a mistake, but you went through with the plan anyway? As I walked down that aisle, my mind was racing back and forth, but I quickly dismissed all those thoughts and became excited in anticipation of my marriage to the person I would spend the rest of my life with.

It was not long after our marriage, I discovered, this is not what I thought it would be like. We were two totally different people living in the same house, with different goals, dreams, and values. When they say love is blind, believe me it is true. I feel we both knew we had made a mistake, but as many wives can attest, you are determined through prayer and commitment and sacrifice, that you can change things. My husband had always been a very sweet, gentle man. It wasn't long before that, he had turned into someone that I did not recognize…a total stranger. He began to have affairs with other women, staying out late and drinking more. I remember one of my close friends called me *at the very time* he was drunk and knocking on her door. Of course, she did not let him in. I thought I was dreaming! You begin to examine yourself and feel as though you are not good enough; you are not pretty enough. What must you do to change? What am I doing wrong?

I knew it could not be the way I took care of the house. I loved to cook, so I would cook beautiful meals, and I always loved a beautiful table setting. I was raised to wash and keep the drawers neat. I remember I would buy nice underwear, shirts, and different things for my husband. I even ironed his shorts if they were wrinkled so they would fold nicely in the drawer. I was prepared by my mother's example to always keep my husband's clothing neat and clean. I know today, we live in a different day and time, however, this was my upbringing. So, I would sit and ponder in my mind: What could be bringing on this great change?

The Good, The Bad, The Ugly

Remember not the sins of my youth, nor my transgressions: according to thy mercy remember thou me for thy goodness' sake, O LORD.

Psalm 25:17

My husband began to drink excessively. I was never a big drinker, but I tried to at least go to the clubs with him. He loved to gamble and began staying out late gambling. It became an addiction. I remember one night, I went to the club; I was drinking *Seven-Up*, and there were three soldiers, I guess on leave from the army base in Tacoma, sitting at the table across from us. The men happened to turn and smile at me. By this time, my husband had quite a few drinks in him. He was a jealous man and so when he stood up, and began to walk toward them, I stood up too, only I made it to the door and out. After being in a relationship with someone, you begin to recognize the signs when something is about to happen. I had become accustomed to his behavior when drinking. I did not have my car keys, so I walked home that night which was just about five miles, because I knew there was going to be a fight.

When my first child Sherrell was born, it did not get better, but worse. My husband's gambling and drinking increased. Let me stop and share something with you: Ladies/Men; please do not live with the false belief that you can change a man or a woman. We have not been given the power to change people. You cannot make someone love you. You cannot make someone quit an addiction, whether it is alcohol, drugs, gambling or fornication. People change because they have a desire to.

They see something within that they realize is not right and *then* they will make up their minds to change. If they do not see the wrong, they will never seek to change. God cannot and will not force you to do anything. He is a God who has given us the greatest gift we could ever possess, and that is the Freedom of Choice. We owe it to ourselves to recognize what's non-negotiable in relationships, so we don't end up resentfully sacrificing our needs, while secretly hoping the people we're with will make it worth our while.

Yes, we desire and try to change our spouses, not realizing there are others out there who would accept your love and value you, just as you are. However, when infidelity, verbal as well as physical abuse, is involved in a relationship, it not only results in emotional trauma but life-threatening experiences. If we would accept the fact that two cannot walk together in covenant relationship when there is no appointment of an agreement.

Ladies/Men: You deserve to be happy in your relationships. That starts with choosing to be with people we'd never want to change. Many feel they can stay in an abusive relationship and pray until the person changes, and that works many times, but if you are not joined together by God, you have no foundation to stand on in your prayer. Two wrongs cannot make a right.

I remember one night, while I was in my bed, I had a busy day and was exhausted. By now, I had my second child, Debra. My beautiful girls were in their beds sleeping. I was suddenly awakened with my husband's knees in my chest, choking me and cursing. He was behaving like a crazy person. I smelled alcohol on his breath and I could not get him to stop. He was constantly repeating something that I could not understand. I set my mind on JESUS and concentrated on the blood. I pictured Jesus at the Cross, when the soldier pierced Him in His side; I saw the blood running down and I set my focus on that blood…I could hardly breathe. I thought I was going to die, but I kept seeing the blood. I could not speak, and I was trying to get some air in my lungs to breathe. *The blood, the blood…*I kept saying in my mind, *the blood of Jesus*. Suddenly, my hand shot up to his forehead and the power of God knocked him backward. It was almost like an unseen hand picked him up and threw him off the foot of the bed to the floor.

When he regained his senses, he ran out of the house and I did not see him for about a week and a half. He and his friend had gone to his sister's home in California. I found this out after he returned home. When he left, he took his paycheck with him and there was no money in the house for food. I was working in the salon at my mother's house during this time. Four customers called and booked appointments to get their hair done. God provided for my family in a great way! At the time, I had no idea where my husband was. I decided while he was away I would go before the Lord in prayer for direction. One evening while in prayer, I had a vision of my husband sitting in a chair at his sister's house playing cards. I saw the angel of the Lord descend down upon that table. When the angel's foot touched the table, my husband fell backward out of the chair. I had never seen anything like this before. I did not understand what the meaning of this was. My husband called and asked if he could come home. I let him. He was scared to get on the road because of the experience he had in his sister's kitchen. I assured him he would arrive safely. He never mentioned the experience.

It was not until he returned home that his friend told me what had happened that night. I asked him what time it was, it was the *exact* time I was in prayer. The power of God is amazing!

I had an awesome father-in-law. I remember one beautiful morning, he called me and asked me to meet him at the hall where he went out to work. I had no idea what he wanted, but I got in my car and met him at the hall. He asked me to take him to the bank. He wanted to make a deposit. So, as I turned into the parking lot of the bank, he asked me to come in with him. So, I followed him into the bank. He said, "I am going to open up an account in your name and I do not want you to tell anyone, not even your husband." He said, "I always want you to have access to money for you and the kids." He opened an account for me that day and deposited five hundred dollars. He said, "Each week, I will put some money into this account. Don't be afraid to use the money as you please. This is between you and me." I will always be grateful to him for that because he knew what situation I was in from time to time.

Women: I plead with you to not stay in an abusive relationship. It could cost you your life. God never intended for you to be abused and used as a punching bag. He didn't always hit me either; but, twisted my arm in front of my parents and playing rough, by pulling on my neck and hands. Those were embarrassing moments that I endured in front of others.

Many women have become unhealthily codependent...you cannot think for yourself. You have come under the control of the person, to the point that fear has taken hold to your very being. You don't value who you are as a woman. You have been stripped of your identity. Well, I am here to tell you that you can reclaim your freedom of mind, at the Cross of Jesus.

He paid the price for your freedom over two thousand years ago. Christ suffered harsh abuse, so you would not have to go through it.

I could share many incidents where my life was in danger. I remember one incident, when my husband was under the influence of liquor, while driving across Lake Washington's Floating Bridge. He was dangerously speeding…up to almost 85-90 miles per hour. He was so full of anger and alcohol, shouting and cussing, "I'm going to kill you. We will both die". It was only God who spared our lives that night.

I remember a time that my husband was so drunk with rage. He waved a gun in my face, threatening my life. I believe alcohol and drugs were the prescriptions he was taking to hide the pain in his life. It was a temporary fix that was taking a toll on his life as well as mine.

The question is asked: Were there any good times? Yes, there were. There were times of laughter…special times when our friends were over. Especially, in the first year or so of marriage. His best friend's wife and I were also best friends. We were close and did everything together. I do not know what we would have done without each other in those years. Thinking back, I believe as I stood in that church, with my arm in my father's, the day of my wedding, preparing to walk down that aisle, is when I could have made the difference in both our lives. We were both young, high school sweethearts, but not meant for marriage to one another. We came from different backgrounds. We had different goals and different desires for our children. We were not compatible in any sense of the word. Compatibility is one of the most important necessities in marriage. I was not raised to live in poverty, spiritually, physically or mentally. My parents taught us that we were children of the

King, so you always carried yourself with dignity. You always dressed nicely. We were taught that we represented the ONE and only God, therefore we exemplified this from the inside out.

When you are connected to the wrong thing, situation, business, man, or woman, it is like trying to walk with *noticeable* gravel in the soles of your shoes; you can walk, but you are going to have some pain.

You would have thought that I would have left…after all the abuse. No, I was still hoping our marriage would change. You see…I was still in love…in love with the man I had created in my mind that did not exist.

There were so many times I experienced verbal and physical abuse. I do not believe this book could contain the years of misery my husband and I endured. I say we both suffered through those years because he had to be a miserable and unhappy man to inflict that much abuse.

Returning Home

But in their distress they turned to the LORD God of Israel, and they sought Him, and He let them find Him

2 Chronicles 15:4

Because of the conflict and emotional pain in my marriage, I made the decision to recommit my life to Christ. I still felt prayer would make a difference. You see I had rededicated my life to Christ. I was in a spirit-filled church, and the expectancy I had for change in my relationship was high. I invited my pastor over to counsel us. My husband did not want the pastor to come to our home, but eventually, he gave in to my persistence in asking. He came and it was a beautiful time of sharing. I did not realize the pain we both were carrying. After pouring my heart out in that meeting, I realized it was as though I was speaking Greek. I remember him saying afterward, "You live in a fairytale world. This is the real world." I guess he was right. However, nothing changed in our marriage; on the contrary, it got worse.

Looking back, I remember the night I made the decision to return to my faith all the way as though it was yesterday. I was lying in my bed and I was so unhappy. The girls were asleep in their bedroom. My husband was out with his friends drinking and partying. Nothing interested me on TV. I was so restless. I tried reading, and I couldn't concentrate. As I laid in my bed that night, the Holy Spirit began speaking to me. "Delores, aren't you ready to return to me?"

I immediately started praying as if my life depended upon my decision; it really did. I felt the presence of God all over me.

His peace was like a river flowing softly; His presence was back. I asked Jesus to forgive me for turning away from Him. I asked Him to come back into my heart, and I asked Him to refill me with the precious Holy Spirit. I knew I needed the Power of God in my life to stand the test I would have to conquer, because of my decision. I began to feel His presence as thick as molasses, pour over me. I was just inhaling the intoxicating aroma of the Holy Spirit. Oh, He is here! He has heard my cry! What joy! What peace!

When all of a sudden, abruptly the sound of the phone piercing through the silence of the night interrupted my thoughts. It was like an invasion of my privacy. I thought who in the world is this? It was pretty late. I reached over and picked up the phone. “Hello, "Hi De, do you know where our husbands are?" I was so disturbed. At that moment, I didn't care where they were. I said exactly that and hung up the phone and immediately tried to recapture the presence I had previously experienced before the interruption of the phone.

I was filled with great anticipation. I begin to praise the Lord and praise and praise. I could not stop praising Him. I was feeling the sweet embrace and comfort of the Father for His presence was stronger than at first. Have you ever stood at the entrance of a place, so excited, nervous, yet ready to step across the threshold, to enter into a place you have never been before? Or partially opening a gift, having untied the ribbon on the box; as you are lifting the top off the box, and removing the tissue to get the gift out? Well, that is the excitement I felt that night. I knew it was just one more step and I would be there. I wanted to speak in my prayer language. I was entering the Secret Place of the Highest. I was desperate for Him. My tongue was released!

RING! That phone... again. It was more piercing than before. I felt like someone getting ready to drink a cold, refreshing drink of water, and someone coming in and snatching it out of their hand.

I reluctantly answered the phone. It was my friend again. "What is wrong with you?" she said, "You hung up in my face. Did something happen? You don't sound right." I said I'm really busy, I am fine. I will call you back later." After assuring her I was ok, I hung up. You have to understand her concern. My husband and her husband were best friends, as she and I were also best friends. They were always together, and she was experiencing in her marriage the same abuses and trauma as me. So, she knew wherever one was, you could be sure the other one was also there. All right, Lord! Here I go again! I started praising my Lord again, wanting to capture that place we had left off. Then, revelation: Get rid of that phone! I could have taken it off the hook, but it might start beeping. You see technology wasn't as advanced as it is today. We had those long phone cords that would tangle, and we had to always untangle them. So, what did I do? I took the phone and put it in the refrigerator and closed the door. I know that might sound funny and ridiculous, but I was desperate, and I didn't want to see that phone or hear it again that night.

I returned to my room got in bed, opened my mouth to regain my flow of praise, and before I could, I began speaking in my prayer language. Hallelujah!!!

I cannot say how long I spoke to my Father in my prayer language. It was amazing. He flooded my soul with His love and grace. He revived me and poured the oil of healing deep within my very soul. When I finally came up for air, I ran to the refrigerator and got the phone and called my mother. In between shouts of praise and tears of joy, I shared my return to Jesus, and the overwhelming love that was overflowing in me. She told me Johanna and she had been praying for me for quite a while. They had joined in the prayer of agreement.

I hung up and called Johanna, my mother-in-law. We had an awesome time on the phone thanking the Lord. I could not sleep, I was on cloud nine, I can't explain the love and joy I felt for Jesus. I guess I must have dozed off because I was suddenly awakened with the sound of the doorbell. A quick glance at the clock revealed the time was a little past 4:00 a.m. I went to the door and asked who was there and recognized my husband's voice. I guess he could not find his keys. He had been drinking as usual, but that didn't bother me. I was so excited that I shared with him what had happened to me. I was talking so fast, I didn't even care how he was looking at me like I was crazy. Well, he wasn't as happy as I was. To put it bluntly, he wasn't happy at all. Nothing could erase the joy I had. I told him I loved him even the more. He just shook his head, took a shower and went to bed.

I had picked up a bad habit those years being away from God, and that was smoking. Well, when my husband came to bed he lit two cigarettes and handed one to me. I said," no thank you, I have quit smoking." He could not believe that so he started blowing smoke into my face, but a strange thing happened; I couldn't smell the cigarette. He continued not believing I was finished with that filthy habit, but I never smelled the cigarette. I was delivered.

Three days had passed since the Lord had restored my life. When I went outside the grass looked greener, the sky looked bluer, everything seemed new including me. I went over to my parents' house that afternoon, and I was just sharing what the Lord had done for me when my brother came in. He had a cigarette in his hand, and I remember him inhaling and blowing out the smoke, and I screamed, "I smell smoke." My brother looked at me strangely and said, Yeah, "I'm smoking." I explained to him what had happened. For the first time in three days, I smelled the smoke from the cigarette. He was not saved but he rejoiced with me, then he put out his cigarette. I was truly free and never picked up another cigarette from that day to this day.

Your Home Will Never Be the Same

You intended to harm me, but God intended it for good to accomplish what is now being done, the saving of many lives.

Genesis 50:20

We had a meeting for three nights at our church. My mother-in-law was going to attend the services with me. Let me say this: I adored this woman. We were extremely close and talked daily. We prayed together. I would pick her up and take her to work every day. She was, next to my mother, the sweetest person I have ever known!

The services were anointed, and the Word being preached was amazing. People were coming to the Lord and healings were taking place in every service. At the close of the second night of service, the evangelist encouraged us to fast and pray the next day. It would be a miracle service. He asked us to bring someone who needed a miracle. He also asked that we bring something of our loved ones that was personal. He was going to pray over it and believe God for a miracle for those who could not attend the meeting.

That next night, I picked up Joanna, my mother-in-law, and she asked if I had remembered to bring something personal of brother's? That is the name she called her son. I said, “No, I forgot”. She said, “Well I did. I found something he had in the house years ago.”

As you entered the church, you could feel the presence of God. The weight of the anointing was present because they had been praying for this miracle night. The service started with praise, which laid the foundation for the message that was shared from the book of Acts 19:12. "So that even handkerchiefs and aprons that had touched him were taken to the sick, and their illnesses were cured and the evil spirits left them."

The minister prayed for many to be healed, and we saw the manifestation of the Lord that night. He had everyone that brought something to pray over, come to the altar. Joanna pulled me up and said, “Come on let's get in line”. I will never forget that night. As we went through the prayer line, the minister anointed whatever was brought from loved ones who needed a miracle, whether physical needs, emotional, or financial. When I passed through the line he stopped me and looked straight into my eyes and said, "Your home will never be the same after this night." I was so excited and so glad she had brought the garment for prayer.

Little did I know what I was going to experience. Truer words have never been spoken, as that which came out of the minister’s mouth. You have in your mind a certain way God is going to move. You expect Him to come from the South and He comes from the North. His ways are higher than ours. We can never figure the Lord.

Well, that night, as I drove Johanna home, I was meditating on the message. As I glanced at the girls, they were sleeping so peacefully, in the back seat. I thought the residue of anointing from the service is hovering over them. They looked like two little angels breathing softly in a rhythmic sound.

I was looking forward to a beautiful night's rest. My husband was working the night shift and would not be in until late. I was very tired because I got my hair done early that morning and then went to town to catch a sale on some shirts at this new men's store downtown. I bought my husband two shirts. I took it upon myself to buy all his clothes because he rarely shopped for himself.

I put the girls to bed and went to bed myself. Sometime, in the early morning, around 2:30 a.m. my husband came home. He woke me up, startling me, by hitting me like a madman. He said, "You are spending money on men and wasting money on your hair... that is not necessary. I was protecting my face, trying to avoid his hands from hitting me. I did not know what he was talking about, and after being dragged out of the bed, I was just trying to keep him off me. My oldest daughter, Sherrell woke up with all the yelling and cursing and fighting. She was screaming "Leave my mother alone!" I thank God that Debra was only eight months old and still sleeping. I think God just breathed a deep sleep on her because I do not know what he would have done in the state he was in.

Sherrell tried to pull him off me; he pushed her away. I was trying to reach for the phone to call my dad, He knocked me away from the phone. I screamed for Sherrell to get the phone and call her grandfather. Then, he yanked the phone out of the wall. I do not know how long this went on, but I know it was *hours*. Every time I tried to get away from him, he would pull me back. Sometime in the morning, it all came to a halt! I knew it was over. I knew it was time for me to take my girls and get out of that house. I did not understand the reason why all this was happening. I grabbed some clothes while he was walking back and forth telling me to get out. All the time, I knew I would never return to this house again.

Picking up my baby and grabbing the hand of Sherrell, who was crying uncontrollably, I headed down the stairs. I got halfway down the stairs and he called my name, and these are the words he said to me: "Delores, I may beg you to come back to me, and ask forgiveness, but if you do, eventually I will kill you." It was the voice of a demonic spirit. I turned and for some reason, I realized there were seven more steps to walk down before I reached the driveway to my car.

When I started the first step, fear fell off me; with the second step, control left me; with the third step, accusation left; with the fourth step, rejection left; with the fifth step, pain left; with the sixth step, imprisonment was gone; and with the seventh step, *all the love* I had for him was *gone*. When I got in the car, I was free. Freedom *surrounded* me! I cannot explain what I felt, but it was over!

It wasn't until months later I found out why he was in a rage of anger. When my husband came in that early morning from work, he scoured through my purse and looked at my checkbook, to see what I had written. He hated it if I wrote a check to the church. I never wrote checks for my tithes and offerings because he was totally against giving finances to the church. I only gave out of my salary. He saw the two checks I had written; one for my hair and the other for the men's store where I had bought his beautiful shirts. He thought I wrote this check to a man. The name of the store was the owner's name, therefore, the check was written out to him. All I know is, it was a terrible night, but was also the night my total and complete deliverance came. *Who the son sets free, is free indeed!*

Did it have to come to this? That is the question I asked. No, I believe not. However, on the other hand, maybe it took this for me to realize that this was not my destiny. I had settled in my heart that this man would come to know the Lord as his Savior, and deliverance from all the habits would leave, while I was still married to him. That was not going to happen.

Physical abuse is not bound by age, socioeconomic status, race, ethnicity, sex, sexual orientation, gender identity, religion or nationality; it exists in all communities. Contrary to popular belief, physical abuse is not simply a maladjusted person's occasional expression of frustration or anger, nor is it typically an isolated incident. Physical abuse is a tool of control and oppression and is a choice made by one person in a relationship to control another.

• More than 10 million Americans are victims of physical violence annually.

• 20 people are victims of physical violence every minute in the United States.

• 1 in 3 women and 1 in 4 men is a victim of some form of physical violence by an intimate partner during their lifetimes.

• 76% of intimate partner physical violence victims are female; 24% are male.

• 1 in 7 women and 1 in 18 men are severely injured by intimate partners in their lifetimes.

• Domestic violence accounts for 15% of all violent crime in the United States.

• Domestic violence is most common among women aged 18-24 and 25-34.

• Majority of physical abuse is committed by dating partners rather than spouses.

• More than 75% of women aged 18-49 who are abused were previously abused by the same perpetrator.

• Intimate partner physical abuse has declined 67% since the passage of the Violence Against Women Act in 1994.

• Slightly more than half of intimate partner physical violence is reported to law enforcement. (World Health Organization)

Out of the Ashes I Rise

To appoint unto them that mourn in Zion, to give unto them beauty for ashes, the oil of joy for mourning, the garment of praise for the spirit of heaviness.

Isaiah 61:3

I lived with my parents for a short while, until I found a little two-bedroom apartment across the street from their house. I moved in and settled down to a life full of challenges. This little duplex compared to my house was different as night is from day. Our house, that I fled from, was a beautiful two-bedroom home with fruit trees in the back and a beautiful little garden. My neighbors helped me to plant vegetables.

In this seemingly little duplex, the Lord would introduce Himself to me in a very special way, in a place of such peace, that words could never describe. There were two bedrooms; one for the girls and the other one was for me. There was a table in what we called the living room. There was a dresser with no drawers and a nightstand.

There was so much peace and joy in that little house, that I learned to love it! God was there, and the aroma of His presence was there. My children were out of danger, and I did not have to ever worry about being attacked in the night again. Yes, my husband did ask me to come back to him, but I had tasted of freedom; I was experiencing peace and I would never forget the words spoken on those steps. I was free! I was experiencing Canaan…why return to Egypt? The great part of the whole matter is I had no anger and I had forgiven him and wished him all the happiness life could offer.

I continued transporting my mother-in-law, back and forth to work. She was kind to me and always made me feel welcomed. I will never forget her words to me, “Delores, "Good for you! God never expected you to live like that. There is something He has for you to do, and although I hate this happened, you will always be my daughter." My father- in- law would often tell me, “Please don't stay away from us, you will always be my daughter in law.

I will always cherish those words; they never changed from loving me. My focus was on my children…to give them a life of freedom and to raise them in the fear of God, and never let them experience the horror of what they came out of again. I taught them to love their dad even though there were times he never came to see them. I taught them to buy gifts on Father’s Day and Christmas even though sometimes he would not even come to get the gift. I shared with them it was nothing they had done to cause this separation. It was two adults who came together to produce two beautiful girls…that was the assignment. “Daddy loves you,” I would tell them. “He is just going through some things, but he loves you.” I taught them to pray for him. Today, they have a very close relationship, with their father for which I thank God.

God blessed me and took me through the hard times. At first, single life was quite a challenge, but I learned how to depend on God for everything pertaining to life. It was difficult finding a babysitter for Debra. I remember that I took her to this woman recommended by someone I considered very reliable. Well, one evening after work when I went to pick up Debra, I knocked on the door and the sitter's sister opened the door. I went in and I asked where Minnie was. She said she was taking a nap, so I asked her if she would please wake her because I was going to pay her. I also wanted to ask why she was napping when she was the one who was supposed to be watching Debra. I felt something wasn't right; she reluctantly went and got Minnie. When she came, I realized that Minnie was drunk and her *sister* had been caring for my baby. My baby was only around 12 months old!

Only a mother can understand how I felt when I saw that woman. At first, I wanted to strangle her. Then, I wanted to just break out crying. I didn't know how long this had been going on. I paid her and told her I would not be needing her service any longer. I left that house holding my child to my breast, weeping over what could have happened with this drunk babysitter caring for my child. I went home and just held her in my arms and prayed and thanked God that nothing had happened. I prayed and broke any negative things that had been imparted into her spirit. I broke anything that would cause any dysfunction in her life in her future.

Single parents: I know it is difficult and very hard to raise your children alone, but God stepped in and literally held me, healed my heart and directed me through those difficult years.

I still had to work even though I did not have a babysitter. I lived across the street on 23rd Avenue from my parents, but I figured my parents had raised four children, and should not have to raise their grandchildren. They should be given the respect and honor to ask to have the children over at their request, not at mine. Oh, my mother would have kept the girls every day, which she shared, but I felt this was my responsibility and God was going to help me, and that He did.

I saw what the enemy was trying to do. I had rescued my children from an alcoholic environment while they were in the home with their dad. Now, the enemy was attempting to use the babysitter, who I found to be an alcoholic to have influence over my child. I did not know what she could have been giving my daughter, so she could drink and possibly pass out while Debra was left in the crib. After all, I dropped her off, early in the morning and did not pick her up until I got off work, which was at times after five. I took authority over every demon connected to alcohol and I broke it from my children's' life. You see: The good thing about raising your children alone, is that you are able to put in them what is needed to fulfill their divine purposes on this earth; you're able to raise them up in the fear of God without any distractions in the home, without any other focus that would lead them away from a healthy life. I was determined to dedicate my life to training my girls to be healthy, emotionally, spiritually and physically. Whatever sacrifice I had to make would not be too much, for their well-being. I vowed with the help of God this would be accomplished.

Now let me be clear about one thing here: I do not mean that there are not good God-fearing men in this world. I am saying, while you are single, live a life of holiness and create an environment in your home that is conducive for your children to be protected from the snares of this world. Teach them, that they can conquer any obstacle they would encounter through Christ. Teach your children that they can become whatever and whoever they desire to be with the help of God.

I remember the day when I came to my parents' home the night I left my husband; my father took me outside a few nights afterward. He held my hand, providing me a sense of comfort. I loved my father very much. Sitting with him made me feel everything was right.

"Honey, look up, what do you see?"

I looked up to the sky. It was really dark, and the stars were really bright.

I said, "I see the stars, in the sky."

"Look harder. What do you see?"

I said, "I see the same thing."

"Look up and close your eyes. Now, what do you see?"

He knew I wasn't understanding what he wanted me to see.

"Look beyond the sky and the stars Delores. Look beyond to what you do not see and get a picture of your dreams and visions."

My smile began to widen. My Dad was such a visionary. I appreciated his wisdom.

"You can have whatever your heart can imagine if you can see it in your spirit...never stop at the stars."

I never forgot that, and I never will. Alaska Airlines had a saying: *The sky is the limit!* No! There are no limits in Christ!

Breaking All Legal Ties

If the Son therefore shall make you free, ye shall be free indeed.

John 8:36

After much prayer, the Lord released me. I would now file for divorce…the total release of my freedom. My dad had taken me to the attorney the next day after that horrible night and had taken pictures of the scars on my neck and the side of my face. The attorney took them to court. I was free. These pictures showed the abuse I had experienced on that night. My husband did not show up in court, so everything was quick, and it was finally over.

I know that many people hold true to the belief that you should never divorce. Also, others have the conviction that Christians should stay with their spouses no matter what the situation is. I do not come against your beliefs; if that is what you desire to do, that is your choice. Oftentimes, I think of many women: If they could break out of the womb of the earth, out of their graves, I believe they would share another story. There are many women who have had premature deaths at the hand of an abuser.

I sought the Lord and He heard my cry. I had every legal right to resolve this relationship. I could never say *marriage* because it was *not* a marriage in Christ. My husband had multiple affairs with women for years. He never respected the vows taken on our wedding day. I was left embarrassed often with the many women he had sexual relationships with. The jealousy, accusations, abuses…that was a way of life for him. I thank God for delivering me while I could live to raise my children.

Let me share something with you. At this point of my testimony, when two people come together in a marriage not ordained by God, it causes them to look for happiness oftentimes outside of the marriage. Therefore, it was easy for me to forgive and be healed because I feel he did not know how to just walk away. I can stand before God on that glorious day and say I have never been touched sexually by anyone except the father of my children. I was in love with my husband and I did not have a problem with lust. Believe me: Again, I was not perfect, but that was not one of my imperfections. Unhappy people find comfort in alcohol, drugs, women, men, and whatever means that will give them temporary happiness. Happiness is the result of many happenings. You must have a *happening* every day to be happy. Joy is the result of one happening which took place on the Cross of Jesus.

Many people who are addicted to alcohol try to convince themselves that their disease is not affecting those around them. Anyone who has lived with an alcoholic knows this is not true; alcoholism affects the whole family and it ruins marriages.

I do not place all the blame on my ex-husband, because I must go back to the young girl getting ready to take that step down the aisle when her dad asked: "Honey are you sure?" Maybe if I would have said, “No,” I could have saved us both from a life of misery, I do not really know. However, I shall always be grateful for two of the most awesome young ladies a mother could ever hope for. I must say, if given the choice of living my life differently, I would have to say I would go through it again because I cannot imagine not having my two girls in my life. I would go through the pain again (yes, the abuse also.) So, I thank my ex-husband for the blessing of two wonderful young ladies that have blessed me beyond measure.

I challenge you young ladies: Do not ignore the signs. There are always signs that will be a red light for you to stop and consider. I had signs which I ignored. One of the signs which was evident from the start was the fact we were not compatible. We had different views on life. We were not spiritually connected. The internal dishonesty we held, not admitting to situations that were obvious. Women: You are foolish to believe that your love for the person will conquer all! That notion is far from the truth. I believe that we must seek God for our mate, and He will lead you to the one that is perfect for you. Note: I said *perfect for you*, not perfect. I was far from perfect. I believe there is only one perfect person and that is the Lord Jesus Christ.

I believe in pre-marital counseling. It is amazing what you find out about a person when you sit in counsel.

As a pastor, I will not marry anyone I haven't had six months counseling with. I feel this is important. You can expose many things about each other and avoid many things. This is not saying you will not have problems, but you know more about how to take your differences to God and pray over them. The Holy Spirit is The Great Counselor, and He alone knows everything about you. If your young man/woman does not want to have counsel before the big day, then I would question if he/ she was really the one that you should spend the rest of your life with.

Pursuit of a Dream

But Jesus beheld them, and said unto them, with men this is impossible; but with God all things are possible.

Matthew 19:26

After the divorce was finalized, the court awarded the house to me. The judge was very kind and wanted me to ask for more; however, I just wanted to be free

We had been looking for a house and praying God would make a way out of no way. I also asked God to give me a house that no one ever lived in, located in an area where my girls could walk to school safely. I asked God for a corner store that they could walk to because I remember when I was a young girl I would walk to the store with my brother and buy candy. I wanted them to have some of the pleasures I had growing up. Last but by far not least, I asked that the house be close to my church.

We found this particular house in the exact neighborhood we wanted. After service, we would drive up to the house. It was not for sale, but it was empty. No one had ever lived in it. We would walk around the house and pray that God would give us that house. We were so excited. I was stepping out on faith believing God for a miracle. After going by the house, peeking through the windows, one Sunday morning, when we came down the driveway, there was a gentleman working outside, who I later found out was the builder. He looked up as we drove down the driveway. I got out of the car and approached him. I said hello, introduced myself, and told him I was interested in purchasing the house. He said the house was tied up at the bank and he wished he could sell it, but until he straightened out all the legal situations he could not sell. I asked him could I go in and look at it. He took us in and we knew this was our house. He tried to persuade me not to concern myself with his house because it probably would be years before he would get out of this situation with the bank. The more he talked, the more I knew that it was our house. You see: Everything I have ever received from God, I have had to fight for it. So, I knew it was time to fight.

I asked him if he had a card and he reluctantly gave me his card. I asked him for another one and I wrote my name and phone number on it and gave it to him. I told him I planned to buy the house. He smiled and told me the bank he was dealing with. I asked him to keep my name and if there were any changes to please call me. He nodded and went back to his work and we left praising God.

Every night, the girls and I would thank God for our house. About three weeks later I called him and asked if he was ready to sell? He said no, and quickly, but very polite, he got off the phone. I called him about three more times, however, we never stopped walking around that house and praying. We never saw him at the house again as we would go there every Sunday and pray.

About three months later I got a phone call. Yes, you guessed it. It was the owner of the house. He said, "Are you still interested in my house?" "Yes, I am" I told him. It was perfect timing. I had sold the family house awarded me by the judge. That was also a miracle. When I went to see that beautiful home, our family had once lived in, I was shocked. The beautiful kitchen floor was warped and some of the tiles were sticking up all over. The house had not been attended to and it was so sad. It did not even look like the same house. I remember I went out to cut the lawn which had grown up in weeds. I remember crying as I cut the lawn and asking God why He gave me this house. I used to cut the lawn and take care of the flowers myself. People would knock on the door often asking me about my flowers. The yard was beautiful. I thought it is going to be more trouble to fix than its worth. I had no plans to live in it because I knew if I did I would have to contend with my ex-husband.

As I was cutting the grass and crying, the neighbor's son came out. He walked over to me and said, "Why are you crying?" I said, "Oh, nothing, I'm fine." I quickly wiped the tears away and gave him my attention. He said, "Well, I saw you out here and I have been wanting to get in touch with you because I am getting married and I want to buy your house." Yes, it was perfect timing. He gave me cash and the house was sold. I had been holding the money waiting on the owner to call on our new house.

My father took me to his attorney and we drew up the papers, and God gave me a miracle purchase.

I was reminded of this Scripture after the finalization of the sale:

"I know the plans I have for you says the lord. Plans not to harm you, but to prosper you and give you an expectant end"

Jeremiah 29:11

The Test

But he knows the way that I take; when he has tested me, I will come forth as gold.
Job 23:10

We moved into our new house, rejoicing and excited over how God had blessed us. One night, only about one week after moving in, I came home, pulled into the garage and walked into the house and immediately I knew something was wrong. I had gone to the store to buy some groceries. I put the dogs in the garage because I did not want them wandering around in the neighbor's yard. I had a little cockatoo named Tuffy, and a registered German shepherd named Axel. A young man I worked with raised German Shepherds and had given me one of the young shepherds for the protection of the children.

When I walked into the house, I was shocked at what I saw. Oh, how I wished I would have left the dogs outside. The curtains were blowing from the sliding glass door that was wide open. Chocolate candy was all over the floor (I had been given a box of chocolates when I moved into our new home). My bedroom window was bashed in and glass was shattered all over the carpet. All the clothes in my closet were lying on the closet floor. My jewelry was gone, and the dresser looked like a storm hit it. Yes, you guessed it right. Someone had broken into our beautiful home. There was mud all over my clothes, carpet, and bed. It was horrible. The yard had not yet been landscaped so it was muddy in back. I felt so violated. I called my dad.

"Are the girls ok?"

"Yes, Dad!"

"I want you to do something right now before you call the police."

"What was that?"

"Praise the Lord!"

Now, my dad was not making any sense. "What?"

"Praise the Lord! I am going to hold onto this phone until I hear you praising God."

"Why should I praise God for someone breaking into my home and stealing my things?"

"You are not praising God for someone breaking in. You are praising God for protecting you. You and the girls could have been there when they broke in, and you all could have been badly hurt, if not killed."

Reluctantly, I gathered the girls to me and told them we are going to praise God. We were going to thank God for protecting us. They obeyed because they loved to praise God and dance. I was the one having the problem. But, I obeyed my father and the longer I praised God, the better I felt. Finally, we were laughing and dancing on the chocolate candy, and all the mess on the floor. Debra did not know what was going on anyway. She just started jumping and dancing because she loved to dance. God's presence came in that house and it was glorious. After I returned to the phone, my dad said "Honey I'm on my way. Call the police. I will be there in a little while."

That's when I understood the Scripture:

"Give thanks in all circumstances; for this is God's will for you in Christ Jesus" - I Thessalonians 5:14

It was the first of many tests that would be experienced in this new place God had brought me to:

"Many are the afflictions of the righteous, but the Lord delivereth him out of them all." - Psalms 34:19

The girls loved that little three-bedroom house and called it *the greenhouse.* Little did I know the significance that name would have on my spiritual growth. It was a very wonderful time for me and the girls. We were having so much fun in our new house. We purchased new furniture for each of their rooms. It was so good to see their happy faces.

I had the responsibility of opening the office each morning at 6:00 a.m. I liked the early hours for work because I would get off early which allowed me to spend more time with my girls. We could prepare meals together and have fun times. I always enjoyed the times I had with my girls. They were six years apart in their age. Sherrell was the oldest. Debra was the little drama queen. She was the little actress, always writing plays, dressing in homemade costumes - sometimes wearing my clothes and heels, and anything she could find to entertain us on a weekend. We would sit by the fireplace on a winter night and eat popcorn and watch her productions.

Sherrell, on the other hand, was my little business girl. She was always puttering around in the kitchen creating new recipes which she tried out on Debra and I...except the ones that ended up in the garbage can. She was my little Martha.

So, you can see why I took the early shift.

Single women and single men: If you trust Him and praise Him in all things, there is nothing the Lord will not do for you. He said He would give you your heart's desire. The secret is in the praise.

I was blessed with a babysitter who lived next door. Sister Smith was trustworthy and really loved the children. My children were happy, and I was so thankful, I did not have to worry about them. I put the girls in private school, although I knew it would be a challenge. But God was with me and taught me how to budget. He had promised to supply all my needs according to His riches in glory. And, I truly believed He would keep His promises. Who would have thought for a minute that God would give me a Christian babysitter next door to the house? We were starting a new life, a new journey. Yes, it would be some struggles, but I was connected to the bloodline of Christ; and through it all, I would learn how to trust in Him.

Favor vs. Money

For the Lord God is a sun and shield; the Lord bestows favor and honor. No good thing does he withhold from those who walk uprightly.
Psalm 84:11

One morning, I got in my car, and was unable to put it in reverse; I knew it was time for another car. My mechanic had advised me some time ago to get rid it. He told me repeatedly that it was too dangerous to drive. I was in no position to purchase another car, but I had to do something. I called my dad and asked him to go with me to look for a car. On the way to the dealership, my dad, somehow, got the car to reverse. It worked okay in *drive*, but every now and then, the gears would stick, and I could not back up. He followed me down to the car dealer.

My dad had previously asked me what kind of car I wanted. I told him I wanted a Buick. While driving, I was thinking the car would stop on me any minute. Well, I was okay, my father was trailing me. The more I thought about my money situation, the more fearful I became. I pulled into the Chevy dealership and parked. My dad came behind me but did not say anything. I looked around the car lot and found a car which I thought would work for me and my budget. After test driving the car, I told the salesperson this is what I wanted. We went into the finance office and sat down. My father was silent; I thought that was strange. We proceeded with the business. Long story short: I did not get approved for the car. I was surprised my father did not step in and say I will help you, honey.

I walked outside of the dealership, looked back at the car and said, "Well, I guess I will go home." I didn't like the car *that* much anyway. My dad gave me a strange look.

"I thought you said you wanted a Buick?"

"I did."

"Well, why are we at this Chevrolet dealership?"

"Honestly, I was fearful, so I thought I would get something more practical and in my budget."

"God can approve you for a Buick the same as for a Chevrolet…that car you picked is too small for you and the girls."

"If I did not qualify for the Chevrolet which was less, how in the world could I qualify for the Buick which cost much more?"

My father looked at me and said, "God doesn't care what the car cost. He just wants you to believe Him for what it is you want. "Make up your mind and don't stagger in your faith. Now, let's go get what you really want."

I felt more confident now because I knew my father would help me. We drove over to the Buick dealer. That was the first time I met John. I picked the car I wanted - a brand-new Skylark Buick. I remember sitting down with John in his John's office.

He later went outside to see if he could put my old Chevrolet in reverse. Walking back in the office with frustration, he said, “I can’t back it up.” I chimed in, “neither can I.” John looked at me for a long time and said, “We must get you into a new car. I refuse to let you drive off the lot with that car. I have a daughter about your age and I would never let her drive this car you brought in for trade.”

I left the car lot with a brand-spanking-new Buick, with *no help* from my father. God set it up, so the monthly payments were what I could easily afford. I bought four cars from John over the years. He became a great blessing to me. I learned a great lesson that day that I will never forget: It is not about money. It is all about God's favor.

My World Crumbled

For everything there is a season, a time for every activity under heaven. A time to be born and a time to die. A time to plant and a time to harvest.

Ecclesiastes 3:1-2

In the year 1973, a tragic thing happened that tore my world upside down. I got a call from work to come home right away; my father had passed. I will never forget that day. It was the worst day of my life. My father was everything to me. He was not just a grandfather to my children, but a father. They called him *Daddy Brooks.* He took them to the park to feed the ducks and go fishing. He played with them. He was a father to them, and they loved him like a father. I did not feel my life would ever be the same. Sherrell was 11 years old, and Debra my youngest was five years old.

You know how God begins to speak to you in dreams and visions? Well, the Father had prepared me for the going home of my precious father, but I did not want to accept what I was feeling and sensing in my spirit.

I had a dream of a fish aquarium. There were two goldfish swimming in the tank; one was male, the other female. I saw the male swim over to the right side of the tank with the female. When the female turned and swam away from the male, he very swiftly shot across the tank to the other side. When the female saw him, she swam over to where he was, but there was an invisible screen she could not get through. He kept swimming and never looked back. She tried every way she could to get to him, but she couldn't. I did not understand the dream completely or I was in denial. I am sure it was the latter.

I asked my mother had she prepared for my father's homegoing if he would be leaving; she ignored me - not realizing really what I was asking her. I asked about three or more times within the space of a month or two after the dream.

So, when my boss was waiting for me that afternoon as I was turning the van into the parking lot, I knew what he was going to say. Upon approaching him, I said “It's my father, isn't it?” He said, “yes” and offered to drive me home. I needed to be alone so I told him I would be all right. He was so kind, so caring.

You see, they knew my father because he would bring them sweet potato pecan pies at their request for Christmas each year. They always offered to pay for them, but my father enjoyed seeing how much they and their families enjoyed the pies, so he would never accept the money. He was an awesome baker.

I remember the homegoing services. Mother was trying to be strong. They had been married for many years, and this was going to be very hard for her. The service was beautiful and the church was full. My father knew so many people. He was a well-liked man with a million dollar smile that was contagious. That night, many people were at the house after the funeral. A woman gave her heart to Christ in my family's living room.

My father used to call me every night before he went to bed. He called me the night before he passed and encouraged me to keep the faith. He said "Its Mother. Do not work until your nerves are shot, you are working too hard... let that job go."

You see, my father named everyone. He had a nickname for the girls. He called Sherrell, *Grendel.* When Debra was born he looked at her and said, "She was going to be different from anybody. I'm going to name her *It.*" So, it was: Its mother, Its sister, Its grandmother, and so on.

At that time, I worked at the University of Washington, and they were changing everything on campus because of Women's Liberation. Demonstrations were getting crazy on campus every day. The workload was changing with equal rights for women, so they were having women do the heavy lifting. I worked in the mail room, not with anything heavy, but the pressure was on and it was becoming stressful on campus.

I left my job at the University of Washington and eventually got a job with Alaska Airlines. I prayed that God would open a position at the Airlines because I wanted to show my children the world. I wanted them to see for themselves the different states in America, rather only seeing pictures in a book. I knew if I could get on at the airline because of the benefits, we could travel and stay in the best hotels for little or nothing. I knew I would have to take a cut in pay because I made a good salary at the University. The benefits would make up for the salary decrease.

Enough Is Enough

No weapon formed against you can prosper.
Isaiah 54:17

I did not realize as a single parent I could have so much fun with my girls: We traveled and went to different places and had a ball. God blessed me to put both girls in a private school. It was a challenge, but God was with me. You see, ever since the divorce from the girls' father, I never received child support. I was not wise in my decision. I felt that, if you did not want to take care of your children, I didn't need your help. God would be my help. I would take care of my children without any help from their father. I considered it an honor. That was foolish, but I was young and did not act with much wisdom those days. The children were entitled to child support from their father.

I want to encourage parents who have not filed for child support to do so. Do not be as I was. Also, all fathers who give money to the children on a continual basis, but you do not go through the court system, please keep your receipts. There are many fathers who give, but not through the court and there is no record of your giving, so it is as though you haven't given anything to your children. I want to encourage fathers to make a serious effort to provide at least some child support, even if it isn't possible to provide the full amount. Learn how the child support system in your community and state operates.

In my case, it was a bit different. Their father gave them nothing; not until years later, which I will get to in another chapter. He did not visit them very often. Many times my oldest daughter would buy a gift for the holidays, waiting for her dad to come and pick it up.

One evening, it was raining hard. You know, one of those rains as in Seattle days. My oldest daughter's face was pressed against the window, waiting for her dad to come and get her. You could not tell the rain running down the window from the tears running down her face. I always insisted they give gifts for the holidays, and for his birthday, whether he came to get it or not.

You may ask why I would insist they give gifts. You must remember that was their dad, regardless of how he acted. I always told them your dad really loves you, but sometimes sin causes you to be preoccupied with your own thing. I assured them the day would come when God would move and he would change and cherish their love for him. Their dad had remarried and had a new life with a new family and just did not have the time for his children. I knew one day that would change.

I realize each case is different. I do not mean to put everyone in a mold. I realize, that some relationships will never be restored. If this is your case, direct your children to the Father of Fathers, the One who always is there. He has promised to never leave or forsake them. He said He would be a father to the fatherless - Psalms 68:5.

I remember one morning, I went to get the mail. I had a letter from the Internal Revenue Service. I had a strange feeling that something was wrong. When you see anything from the Internal Revenue Service, it is cause for concern. Just looking at the envelope fear gripped me, and I hadn't even opened the envelope.

Well, I was shocked. They were charging me thousands of dollars because I had claimed my children as dependents. I tried calling them and that was like, trying to reach the president of the United States. I stayed on hold so long I eventually hung up. Yes, you guessed it right. When I finally was able to speak to a human, they explained the girls' dad had claimed them on his tax return and said he was paying for their private school and sending finances on a regular basis. It was a nightmare trying to convince the Internal Revenue Service, even with the paperwork, that he was lying.

Finally, one Saturday morning, I guess the girls thought I had lost my mind. I had been in daily prayer with the weight of this IRS bill pressing me. I went to the mailbox and there was another letter, which was about the fourth one, which was now threatening me...what they were going to do, etc. I got so mad at the devil I took that letter and held it up before the enemy, and I called him out. I went to war in prayer. When I finished, I took that letter tore it up in pieces and opened the door and threw it out and told the devil I dare him to ever come back. I knew the power of prayer. I also knew, that until I began to rise up in my spirit and take control of this situation, which was a spirit of theft and lies, I would be paying something that I should not have been paying for.

In about three weeks, I received a letter saying I owed them nothing. You know The Internal Revenue Service will never say, “I'm sorry we made a mistake,” but that was okay. It was over!!! The enemy was so mad, that I received a phone call from the girl's dad cussing me out because they had sent a letter demanding *him* to pay. Isn't it just like the devil? He gave me nothing for the children, lied on his taxes, then got mad because he was caught in the lie and had to pay.

I later found out from my attorney, that I did not have to go through that stressful time with the IRS. He told me all I needed to have done was to call him, and he would have taken care of it in a matter of minutes. I asked God why He didn't let me know so I could have avoided all the stress those months I went through. His answer was, "I am training you to become a warrior. I am training you how to conquer through the power of prayer."

Victory In the Courthouse

For the Lord God will help me; therefore shall I not be confounded: therefore have I set my face like a flint, and I know that I shall not be ashamed.

Isaiah. 50:7

I found out, I was single yet married. You might not fully understand what I mean, but I had experienced the covering of a Father and the care of a Husband in Christ. I was the Bride of Christ and my relationship with the Lord was growing, and blossoming. I was discovering who I was, more and more each day. My identity had been restored, and I knew I had legal rights as a Child of the King.

I was excited over life itself. I had begun a Bible study group on my job, and many were getting saved. The president of the company had given me the law library for my Bible study. God was good. Then, suddenly, it was like the enemy hit me with an unexpected blow.

I got a subpoena to appear in court. Not only me, but my mother also. The girl's father was taking me to court. For the life of me, I could not figure out what I had done to have to appear in court. I had never been in court in my life except for the divorce and that was in a little room with about three people: the judge, my lawyer, the recording secretary, and myself.

I called my mother and read the subpoena to her. She told me to call the lawyer, which I did. Well, my attorney explained that I was being taken to court because my girls' father wanted the child support the court had stated he had to pay removed. He now had another family and this amount of child support was blocking him from obtaining some property, etc. It was strange because he had never paid child support in the first place. My attorney told me not to worry. My mother did not have to go to court. I asked why her name was down on the subpoena anyway. He later explained that my ex-husband had stated my father left my mother quite a sum of money and therefore I was taken care of, so he should not have to pay anything. Also, I had purchased a very expensive German shepherd, so I didn't need the money.

During this time, my children were getting treatment from the dentist as well as the orthodontist and needed braces, which I was paying for. My insurance covered some but not all. Their father's insurance covered the remainder; however, the dentist nor the orthodontist had received any of the checks sent by his insurance.

The day finally came when we all appeared in court. Because the girls' father had never paid child support, the judge was quite disturbed. However, everything worked in my favor because the judge ruled, that the following day the total owing for all the years he had not paid, he must now be paid by him at court immediately. He would also begin making regular monthly payments of child support to the court. If he missed, they would pick him up and he would be placed under custody. The insurance company was also present that morning, and he had to give to the dentist all the money they had paid which he had pocketed. If I live to be a hundred, I will never forget the judge's face when he looked at me. He said, "Mrs. Kendrick, what do you want? Your ex-husband has many assets, you can have anything you want." Then he read all the property and assets. I really did not want anything but to be left alone to raise my children.

The judge looked at me and tried to persuade me to at least take the property. But again, I assured him I was fine. He then looked at me and said: "In all my years I have sat in this seat, I have never quite met anyone like you." I thanked him, and we left. God was so sweet and thoughtful of me. He set the whole thing up because it really did not make any sense. But God wanted my children to be cared for, as they should have been.

One might say I was foolish to not take it all. But I do not see it like that at all. God is my Jehovah Jireh, (Provider) my Security, He alone is my All and All. All I ever would need was in Christ. It has never been my desire to destroy anyone or seek revenge. The only people who entertain these thoughts and actions are the ones who are not fully healed. I forgave my ex-husband years ago, and in doing so I received healing. I even asked him to forgive me for anything I had done that brought pain in his life. Yes, I am free. I know who I am, and over the years I can attest to the fact that My God has taken very good care of me and my children. I have peace that surpasses all understanding, and I have complete fulfillment and joy. Listen: if you are still holding anger, want revenge because of what someone did to you, you will only cause bitterness to grow inside of your emotions, which places you under the control of another. They are still controlling your life and you are in bondage. Get rid of the root of bitterness and release them to God. Many sicknesses are the result of holding unforgiveness and hate. Believe me: it is not worth it. You say, “I can't release it.” Try this: "While we were yet sinners, Christ died for us." If Christ died for us and forgave us all the sins we have committed, and injustices we have done, how much the more can we forgive others?

How can you ask God to forgive you, if you do not forgive others that have wronged you? So, whether you believe it or not, just speak forgiveness every day until the words eventually become meaningful for you. Then ask the Father to fill your heart with love, and the Balm of Gilead will pour into every part of your emotions and flood you with His healing power.

Transitioning Back Home

For even the Son of Man did not come to be served, but to serve, and to give his life as a ransom for many.

Mark 10:45

My mother was having a difficult time living alone. My dad and mom had been married over 40 years. They had never been separated for any length of time. The only time they were *briefly* apart, was when he came to Seattle to find a place to live; then he sent for us. I was driving back and forth from work across town to be with her every other day, and it was taking its toll on me. I would go to work, come home and feed the girls, drive over to mothers, spend time with her, then drive home and prepare the children for bed after their homework was finished.

Mother had been spoiled by my dad: She never learned to drive. He took her everywhere she went, and she was not handling his absence well at all. I found my health was headed toward a decline and I was tired all the time. I worked in the accounting department at the airlines. After caring for the girls, helping them with their homework, cooking and taking care of the house, then going over to mother's I was exhausted.

I prayed and asked the Lord for directions. Show me what I should do? Sometimes, I stayed with her, but that was not working out. I knew mother would not sell her home and move in with me. All her memories were in that house with dad. Plus, my house was small, with only three bedrooms, and one Jack and Jill bathroom, so we would be too crowded.

After sharing and seeking counsel with my pastor's wife, I knew the best thing to do was to move back home with mother and take care of her because she was getting older and was totally dependent on me. I thank God for my brother Laurice. He would come often to take mother shopping and spend time in prayer with her. He had the patience of Job.

We eventually moved back home. I was not able to get any equity out of the house because I hadn't been there long enough. Mother had four bedrooms, so I got the girls settled into their rooms, and we began our new life with mother. I wish I could say it was fun, but my mother was set in her ways, and used to things being her way. It was a long commute to work, but it worked for the good. I was able to get a lot of time in prayer and there were some awesome times with the Lord in that commute.

A Beautiful Day In Autumn

Beloved, think it not strange concerning the fiery trial which is to try you, as though some strange thing happened unto you.

Peter 4:12

We had been living with mother for some time when things began to change. It was a quiet evening in autumn. The leaves were turning those beautiful colors of orange, yellow and red. Seattle is beautiful in this season. Autumn is my favorite time of year. Many perceive it as a time of death, because the trees are losing their leaves, The fruit is just about all gathered off the trees, and there is a sense of silence in the air. I think of it as *getting rid of the old and preparing for the new.*

Autumn is also a time when birds begin their migration to warmer climates, and animals start collecting food to prepare for the winter. The air is crisp and refreshing as the wind blows against your face.

It was such a day as this that my daughter Sherrell and I left the house to go to the supermarket to do a little shopping for the week's groceries. I had just gotten off work and was happy for the day was Friday, *Oh, happy day!* We parked the car and went into the store, grabbing a cart as we wheeled it in.

We strolled slowly down the aisle observing and comparing the prices of the items on our grocery list, keeping within our budget. When we were just about finished and ready to go to the cashier, a strange thing happened: Suddenly, I froze in my tracks and I couldn't move. It was almost like an invisible force had paralyzed my legs, holding them to the floor, making it impossible for me to pick up my feet. My feet felt like there was a ton of bricks holding them down to the floor.

As I stood there wondering what was going on and thinking how silly I must have looked because I was blocking the aisle with my cart. People were walking around me, trying to figure out why I did not move out of the way so they could at least walk around me. You know how people can look at you and never open their mouths, yet you hear what they are thinking, and it is not very nice. I smiled at them and tried not to look too ridiculous.

It is amazing how fear takes a hold to you and in a few minutes, your mind is thinking every negative thought possible. My daughter was frightened and getting teary-eyed, wondering what is wrong with her mother, and why she has not moved out of the way. I was trying to convince her that mother is okay, I just needed to leave the store. I was frightened myself, but I was trying to hide my concern from her. Finally, after what seemed like forever, I was able to slide my feet using the shopping cart as a brace to get to the front of the store. I left the cart full of groceries in the store and with the help of my daughter, I slowly made it to my car. Now, I must figure out how to bend my knees enough, so I could get into the car. Sherrell was not driving yet. It was very awkward, but with

Sherrell's assistance, I was able to position my body to slide down the back of the seat, to a position on the seat in the car. Now, inside of the car, I managed to drive home. I quickly found out it was not just my legs, but it appeared as if in just a few minutes, my complete body was finding it difficult to maneuver the vehicle. It was difficult to turn the steering wheel because the muscles in my arms were without warning, very weak.

We finally made it to the house. Breathing a sigh of relief, I said "Thank God, we safely made it home." As I pulled into the garage, my mind was racing with all kinds of negative thoughts. I managed to get out of the car, but by now the pain had worsened, and it felt like my loins were locking up in me. After a couple of attempts, I got out of the car lifting my body very slowly.

What is happening to me? Am I dreaming? Little did I know this was just the beginning of one of the greatest tests of my life. No, this was no means a dream, it would become a nightmare.

I tried walking up the steps to the second floor to my bedroom, however, I couldn't lift my feet high enough to the next step. I found it was easier to scoot up the stairs backward on my bottom than it was to try to walk up those stairs. It seemed like 100 steps; however, it was only about 13 altogether. I did not want to alarm my mother by her seeing me in this condition. She was going through enough recovering from her husband's death. After all, this would be just a memory tomorrow, it was all just a bad dream.

Have you ever stood at the foot of a mountain and looked up and wondered how the mountain climbers conquer it? Well, as I reached the side of my bed I thought, “Why did I put those mattresses on that bed?” You see I have always liked a high bed. So, I had three mattresses on my bed which made it very high. My children helped me to get in bed. After taking some pain pills, I finally went to sleep.

The next morning, when I woke up I could not move. My body would not cooperate with what my brain was telling it to do. It seemed, where I was only confined in my legs, the stiffness had moved to my complete body. I couldn't even lean over to pick up the phone which was on the nightstand right next to my bed. I was trying to reach the phone to call in to work, but I couldn't. I tried to force my body to turn towards the nightstand, then I could sort of leap to the phone. It wasn't working. I felt so helpless and frightened, and so alone.

I tried calling my girls who were just down the hall from my bedroom, but I couldn't inhale enough breath to release a cry for help. I found out that it takes energy and it takes breath to get enough strength to be able to call out. Every time I tried to inhale breath, to call my children in the other room, my rib cage would hurt so bad I couldn't cry out. My feeble attempts to cry out for help would just come out of my mouth a mere whisper. I began at that moment to understand how fearfully and wonderfully we are made.

As you breathe in, your diaphragm contracts and flattens out. This allows it to move down, so your lungs have more room to grow larger as they fill up with air. "Move over, diaphragm, I'm filling up!" is what your lungs would say. The diaphragm isn't the only part that gives your lungs the room they need. Your rib muscles also lift the ribs up and outward to give the lungs more space.

At the same time, you inhale air through your mouth and nose, and the air heads down your trachea or windpipe. On the way down the windpipe, tiny hairs called cilia (say: SILL-ee-uh) move gently to keep mucus and dirt out of the lungs. The air then goes through the series of branches in your lungs, through the bronchi and the bronchioles.

I found this to be true: If a fire had broken out in the house, I would not have been able to get out of bed or cry for help.

After a while, my children got up for school and came into my bedroom wondering why mom was not up yet. I am so thankful to God that I trained them to set their alarms and get up early for school and not depend on me to always have to wake them up. They helped me out of the bed and helped me dress. Little did I realize this was going to be the way it would be for some time.

What Have I Done Wrong?

They will have no fear of bad news: their hearts are steadfast, trusting in the LORD.
Psalms 112:7

I finally called into my job that day and told them that I would be in the next day. Next, I began to look in my phone book to call my doctor, to find out if I could get an emergency appointment. I had to find out what in the world was happening to my body. The receptionist, after checking my doctor's schedule for the day, told me to come right in. I managed to get down the stairs without as many problems as coming up the stairs. I checked on my mother and left for the doctor's office. Have you ever wondered why it is, that you can have pain so bad, but the minute you decide to go to the doctor's office, it is not as bad? You have a toothache, then when you get to the dentist office, the toothache is gone.

As I pulled into the parking lot at the doctor's office, I gave God thanks for the elevators because I would never have made it up the stairs. I parked the car and managed to get out, with pain ripping through my complete body, however it was not as bad as the night before. I was able to move a little better, probably because I had taken three of my mother's arthritis pills. I slowly made my way to the elevator to go to the fifth floor. I gave my name to the receptionist and sat to wait for the nurse to call me. I felt that I would be waiting a long time since he was working me into his schedule.

As I sat in that chair, my head was spinning. I was questioning God, asking Him "What had I done for this to happen to me? What is this that is attacking my body? I have children to raise, and I am a single parent. I have to work." The questions were coming so fast that I did not hear the nurse call me to come to exam room. I broke out of my deep thoughts and silenced the voices speaking negative thoughts to me. It is crazy...the many voices that come to your mind...and you listen and communicate with everyone. Finally, I went into the exam room. He thoroughly examined me and shared with me what he feared the diagnosis was, but he wanted to be sure, so he referred me to a specialist. He wasted no time and I was able to go the specialist that morning; he confirmed the doctor's diagnosis. I had rheumatoid arthritis in the worst way and it was all over my body! My immediate response and question was, "Lord why? How did this happen so fast?" And again, "Lord, what have I done wrong? Why is this happening to me?"

It's funny how the enemy always attacks your mind with: *you did something wrong*, or *you are being punished.*

Then, I heard a loud voice in Heaven say: "Now has come the salvation and the power and the kingdom of our God, and the authority of His Messiah. For the accuser of our brothers and sisters, who accuses them before our

God day and night, has been hurled down. (Revelation 12:10).

The enemy, that old devil, accuses the saints, day and night. If it wasn't for the Lord, I believe I would have lost my mind. The Lord spoke, reassuring me that He would never leave or forsake me. At the same time, the enemy was also speaking to me: *"It looks like he has already left you."* I had to reassure myself that this sickness was not brought upon me by God, but it was brought upon me by the enemy because God is not the author of sickness. He is my Healer. He took the stripes on His back for me. The enemy came to steal and kill. He tries to force his will upon you...and I do mean *force* because he tries to force his intentions upon the mind. The organ of thought is the first place he attacks, with his strategy against the Word of God. The enemy will try to make you doubt the Word of God if you listen to him.

I left the office confused and feeling defeated. With all the knowledge of God and His word I had in me, I was communicating with the enemy...something I taught others that you *never* do. I made up my mind later in the day, I was going to defeat this sickness, and I was going to win this battle.

I picked up the prescription the doctor had given me and drove home. The pain pills helped a little. It was not being able to move my legs that bothered me most. After about three weeks, it wasn't only my legs that began to stiffen up on me, but my arms, my fingers, and my feet. It was as if my body was shutting down. It was difficult to find comfortable positions to lay down. I was losing control of my body. This was difficult for me because I rarely got sick; and that was a cold occasionally. I had so much sick leave at work because it was unnecessary to use it.

Coping With Change

The LORD will strengthen him upon the bed of languishing: thou wilt make all his bed in his sickness.

Psalm 41:3

The next few weeks were nightmarish because of the arthritis. I had to get up very early because of the length of time it took to prepare myself for work. There were many things that I began to discover. One, was that there were not many entrances on the freeway, where you did not have to make a real hard turn to get on. I had to locate an entrance to the freeway where you did not have to use your arms to turn so fiercely. I had to find a new route to work. Second, I also realized that I had to be careful to always make sure someone was around if I had to bend on my knees; I might not be able to get up on my own. The joints in my body seemed to lock. It was as though I was almost paralyzed. I could not believe this was happening to me. I had always been a very active person and never had any physical problems, so this was very difficult for me to accept.

I remember one afternoon, we were out of coffee at work, so I went to make some. I picked up the pot to get some water and it slipped out of my hands and crashed on the floor. I was so frustrated I felt like screaming. These were the times I would have to steal away and talk with the Lord and let Him minister to me.

I think one of the most difficult areas for me was not being able to lift my hands in praise to the Lord, and not being able to dance before Him. The joints in my body prevented me from using my limbs in any active way. The doctors would do everything they could to relieve the pain. The medication they gave me did not help; nothing seemed to work. My body became worse each day and the pain lasted for 24 hours. The doctors informed me one afternoon, to begin to prepare my mind to be in an institution by the time I was 38 years old. I would be crippled with Rheumatoid Arthritis. I was becoming weaker and weaker. I started taking pain pills at 12:00 a.m., every three hours so I would be sure to get out of bed.

I thanked God for my girls!!! They would help me to dress each morning, so I could go to work. One of the most difficult things was being able to put on pantyhose. As I look back on it today, I probably could have won the world's funniest video when trying to put those stockings on. It took me about two hours to prepare for work. In today's world of change, it wouldn't have been a problem because nude legs are fashionable, but not then. God was good to me because I opened the building every morning at 6:00 a.m., and I never was late.

Gold: Oh, Happy Day!

But thanks be to God, which giveth us the victory through our Lord Jesus Christ.
1 Corinthians 15:57

The pain from the arthritis became so bad that I could not lift my arms any higher than my waist. I could not bend my knees. I could not walk fast and running was out of the question.

After some time, I was not able to find any relief from my pain even with my treatment. My doctor called one morning with what he felt was good news, the answer for all my problems. The doctors had found a drug that would help me to function in a normal way. They explained it was not a cure-all, but they assured me I would feel a lot better than I had been. They found a drug called. *gold.*

Gold therapy was one of the first treatments for rheumatoid arthritis, Gold is a DMARD, or disease-modifying anti-rheumatic drug, but it has been replaced as an rheumatoid arthritis treatment with newer, more effective, and better tolerated biologic and non-biologic DMARDs. Side effects can be extremely irritating. Although gold injections can be effective for some people, their use has declined dramatically in the last 20 years due to the severe side effects and thanks to the advent of more effective and better tolerated biologic and non-biologic DMARDs, such as Trexall (methotrexate).

They began to inject large doses of gold into my system. They wanted to give me a year's supply. Well, I will tell you almost immediately I felt better. The doctors failed to tell me about the side effects. I probably would have consented to take the gold shots anyway because I was so tired. Pain drains you of all strength and energy. The pain from rheumatoid arthritis is a continual nagging and aching pain. It attacks the joints and never lets up. It also has cousins that are connected to its pain: irritation, a sharpness of speech toward others, low tolerance, anger, no patience, fear, lack of sleep, and many other things that attached itself to the pain.

If it wasn't for Christ in my life, I think, I would have given up, but I had the comfort in knowing that God was still with me, regardless of how I felt. Yes, it was definitely a challenge. Sometimes, I would think: “I'm conquering this illness.” Other times I would think, “I will never conquer this, I'm too tired.”

Every week I would go into the office to receive my shot of gold. My doctor found an office close to my job so that I could run in at lunchtime to get the shots. You could never imagine how it felt to once again be able to bend my knees in prayer and to lift my arms in praise. Oh what a joy that was! I was like a little girl who had just come back to life. Before, I could only wear one pair of shoes because of my swollen feet. Now, my feet had gone down from being swollen. My fingers had been disfigured so I couldn't wear rings, now I managed to put my rings back on. It was wonderful to open the car door without using a pen, which I always kept with me, because I had one of those car doors that you had to press the button with your thumb in order to open the car, and my fingers were not strong enough to do that. I would place the pen between my thumb and the rest of my fingers. This way, I could write and function on my job. I could not bend my fingers. I also was unable to open the files at work with my fingers unless I used a pen or pencil.

Oh, how I praised the Lord for the miracle of medicine. I decided to take the girls and my mother on a vacation. My mother had never been back to her place of birth since she had left, many years before. I decided to take her and the girls to visit her family. We left for Texas and we had a wonderful trip. I was able to walk without pain and drive the car we had rented. It was a wonderful trip.

We went to Shreveport, the city where my mother was born in Louisiana. We also went to Dallas, where I took the children to Six Flags Over Texas. It was awesome!

I felt as though I had been physically born again with a new body. I was so grateful to God for using the doctors for me to once again function as a normal human being.

The Job Experience

But He knows the way I take; when He has tried me, I shall come forth as gold.

Job 23:10

I stared out of the window of the plane, as we were returning from Texas. We were cruising at 37,000 feet headed home. I watched another jet flying the opposite direction. It was peaceful and quiet because most of the passengers were asleep. The girls were nodding, about to go to sleep for the long flight home. Yes, it had been a beautiful trip. I dozed off and was awakened with a little itching in my left hand. It got worse! Then, my right hand began itching. Finally, this itching became unbearable, as I felt it in the palms of my hands, and then burning in my feet. I didn't know what was going on. I woke my Mother and showed her how the palms of my hand were red as blood. My mother told me that it might be from the heat in Texas; it was extremely hot. I was not used to 90 degree weather. We arrived home, but the itching in my hands and the burning in my feet never stopped. I thought it would after a few days in Seattle's cool climate.

The next morning, the burning persisted so I made an appointment with my doctor only to find out that I was having a reaction from this drug. Yes, the doctors forgot to share with me the side effects of this drug. He immediately took me off it and apologized for not telling me the side effects of gold. I left the office thinking, since I was off the drug, the itching and burning would soon stop. In about two weeks, I broke out in this rash, which is also one of the side effects. The itching increased and I thought I was going crazy. Under my armpits and around the neck area, this rash was very noticeable, so I went to my dermatologist. He took one look at me and asked me what in the world I had put in my body. I began to explain to him about the rheumatoid arthritis and my doctor prescribing me gold, and this was the side effect from it. He was so angry, he made me promise to not take any more shots. Of course, I had already stopped taking the gold injections because of the side effects.

The dermatologist began treating me for the itching and burning and the rash right away. Little did I know, this was about to turn into a nightmare. This would be one of the greatest challenges I have ever experienced in my life.

If I Perish, I Perish

When I lie down, I say, when shall I arise, and the night be gone? And I am full of tossing to and fro unto the dawning of the day.
Job 7:4

The high praises of the Lord were awesome as the congregation entered worship that beautiful Sunday morning. What a joy to be able to lift my hands in freedom and enjoy the presence of the King. I cannot imagine any greater joy than singing and dancing before the God of the whole universe. The freedom from pain was wonderful! I shared my testimony with those who worked with me, and those I fellowshipped with, and how I had been healed through the miracle of medicine.

You see, the prescription given by the doctor had begun to stop the itching. I still enjoyed the freedom from the pain of arthritis because the drug was still in my system. At this point, I was able to function and live a normal life.

My doctor had put many months of this drug in my system, so I wouldn't have to come in every week. When I think about that now, I realize how foolish that was. The only way to really understand is to experience pain as I had. You will agree to anything to be able to function from day to day.

Little did I know, that I was getting ready to experience something that would challenge my faith like nothing I had ever imagined. I took the medication that the dermatologist gave me, and I stopped going to the specialists. For about four weeks, I experienced such awesome freedom in my body, and then I noticed that all the symptoms slowly began to return. I began to experience tightness in my joints once again.

It was subtle. The pain did not happen overnight, but gradually I began to feel my body returning to the place I thought I had left for good; tightness in the joints, restless in bed, finding a position to be comfortable, slowing down with my steps and not being able to move fast.

The rash became worse and began to spread over the sensitive areas of my body. It became really visible. It would itch so until I could barely stand it. If that was not enough, there was a fluid that was oozing from the rash, which seemed to focus on every sensitive area of my being. There was a foul smell that came from the fluid that I could not control.

When I went to work, I had to place a towel under my armpits so I would not offend anyone because of the odor from the fluid. I could not use deodorant because that would irritate the skin. The rash broke out on my face and neck. The rashes were so irritating. I always wore a scarf, trying to hide as much of the rash as possible. I changed the towels under the scarf around my neck four times a day because of the fluid coming from the rash. I later found out this was the medication emptying out of my system. This was the gold medication which was injected into my body. The doctor had tried to put quite a large supply in my system so I wouldn't have to go to him for shots every week. I realized this would take some time for all the drugs to empty out of my system.

Although the prescription the dermatologist gave me did wonders, it was difficult to stop the oozing of this medication and the smell that came with it. I did not know which was worst, arthritis or the rash, which eventually began to spread all over my body. It was very difficult to hide it, and so I began to wear clothes with long sleeves and high necks.

The arthritis eventually returned because I had stopped taking the drug. But, the draining from the drug became worse. Once again, I could not use my hands. I took my rings off because my hands had swollen as they had before. My feet had also swollen again, and I could not fit into my shoes. It appeared as if the arthritis had returned worse than before. It hurt to blink my eyes or walk. It was difficult to hold a coffee cup, or anything in one hand because I could not bend my fingers. Isn't it amazing how we either ask the questions, "What have I done wrong?" "Lord, what are you doing to me?" Where are you God…I can't hear you, Lord. I can't take this anymore." Even the questions returned.

God is not the author of sickness and disease. He is our Healer. He is our Deliverer. "I am the Lord that healeth thee."

"Surely, he hath borne our griefs, and carried our sorrows: yet we did esteem him stricken, smitten of God, and afflicted. But he was wounded for our transgressions, he was bruised for our iniquities: the chastisement of our peace was upon him, and with his stripes, we are healed"
Isaiah 53:4-5

The doctors had done all they could do. They asked if I would come in because they had discovered another drug with fewer side effects. I decided to put myself in the hands of my God totally and completely.

My Personal Party with Pity

And there were four leprous men at the entering in of the gate: and they said one to another, why sit we here until we die?
2 Kings 7:3

We had a tent crusade at our church which lasted seven nights. As I sat in the service that first night, trying to concentrate on the Word of God, all of a sudden, I could feel the fluid draining out of my body. My pastor's wife gave me the keys to go up to her house and clean the area of my body so it would not offend anyone with the foul smell from the fluid. She lived on the property, so I just walked up the hill. She knew the battle I was fighting and was in constant prayer for me.

I was always prepared with towels, and with a change of clothing which I kept in the car in case of emergencies. I went to the car and got some fresh towels and a blouse and hurried as best I could up the hill to her house. I washed up and returned to the meeting.

I was not going to the doctor anymore, but I went to the dermatologist for the cream I used which helped a lot. He explained that the rash would not completely go away until all the drug had emptied itself out of my body, which was going to take some time.

The more I praised God, it seemed the sicker I became. I remember one day, I did a foolish thing. You see, I love to work in the yard, plant flowers, and watch them grow. I had bought some petunias and some lobelias. I was out on the lawn working in the flower bed enjoying a beautiful sunny day.

We lived right on the main street in Seattle, and the bus stopped right in front of the house. I guess I got a little carried away out there, when I realized the sun was going down and I had been in the yard working for hours. My children were spending the night with someone, so they were not home. I thought I better get up and call it a day. When I tried to move, I had been sitting for so long in that position, I could not move. Anyone who has ever had any problems with their joints know what I mean. Well, I couldn't move, and it was getting a little dark. The bus was dropping off their passengers and here I sat in the flower bed. You can imagine how silly I looked.

I must have sat out there for nearly an hour. Finally, I told the Lord: "Please help me." If I could just get in a position to crawl, I could reach the steps, and that would help me to have something to hold on to. Long story short, the Lord heard my cry and I was able to crawl to the steps and hoist myself up on a step and I managed to stand up. Whew! I promised I would never be that foolish again.

I thanked the Lord, for "He is a present help in the time of trouble." (Psalms 461)

I began asking God, "What must I learn from this illness?" For one thing, I was developing a new level of respect for the members of my body, for I was fearfully and wonderfully made. (Psalms 139:14) When one part of my body wasn't functioning properly, it affected my entire body.

"In my distress, I called upon the Lord, and cried unto my God: he heard my voice out of his temple, and my cry came before him, even into his ears"
Psalms 18:6

I was beginning to understand and see how important the members of the Body of Christ are to one another. Jesus prayed that we would be one. When one member in the church suffer and have pain, whether emotionally or physically we should feel them for we are one body in Christ. We are divinely connected spiritually (John 17:21). All the members of this body are necessary to function properly, and if one of us is hurting it should affect us all. We must honor the lesser member because we need one another. I began to pray for God to give me a love for the body of Christ, like never before. However, at the same time, I was blaming God for my situation and didn't realize it. I was having a real pity party. We tend to blame God for all our misfortunes. I wanted to dance before Him, and clap my hands and glorify my God which is in Heaven, so, "Why don't you heal me, Lord?"

God broke through my pity party, and spoke to my heart and said, "Delores you can praise yourself out of this situation or you can sit here until you die." He reminded me of the two lepers in II Kings 7:3 where they said. "Why sit we here until we die, we might as well get up and pursue."

The Holy Spirit reminded me of Paul and Silas who were in prison. They began to praise the Lord in the midst of their pain, in the midst of their dark place and in the midst of their imprisonment. (Acts 16:16-40)

It felt as if I was in prison, for sickness had me bound and fear had gripped my heart. " Do you know you can praise yourself out of this condition, Delores? Do you know the power of praise? It is a strong weapon." I began to praise God!

Praise will break the chains that hold you, and shatter every wall that confines you, and deliver you from the enemy of disease. I could not lift my hands, but Lord I will praise you with my mouth. I began to repeat. "I will bless you Lord at all times, your praises shall continually be in my mouth."

Many people ask me, “Don’t you think that is a little much? I mean, you do not have to become fanatical.” Let me stop before I get ahead of myself. My body was in a horrible condition, and God was telling me to praise Him. My praise to Him was not for the sickness, but I was to praise Him in the midst of the sickness. God did not put this sickness on me. While I was fighting for my deliverance, He was going to teach me something in the midst of all this trauma. He was teaching me the power of praise. Yes, I was praising, but as the days went into weeks, and weeks went into months, I was becoming exhausted from the pain. It was a fight.

I was so tired of not seeing any results. Pretty soon, it would be nearly two years since I first experienced this horrible sickness. I was getting weaker in my faith, but I never stopped praising God (Whether I felt like it or not) Sometimes, it was but a whisper.

The Pathway & Key to Victory

God is enthroned in the praises of Israel and He inhabits praise.

Psalms 22:3

One evening, I was home alone again, and I was puttering around in the children's room. I laid on the bed to take a rest for a few minutes. This illness drains your energy, so you can only do a little work at a time. You must take many breaks to finish a simple task.

After laying there for some time, the quietness of the hour was loud, if you know what I mean. It was utter silence in that room, sort of eerie. Then, I felt an unusual presence of the Holy Spirit, which was different…such as I have never felt again to this day. I was lying on my back so I could not see the door of the bedroom clearly, but I felt the Lord come into the bedroom. I did not see Him, but I felt His presence when He entered the room. It was as though He came from the direction of the door. He came closer and closer and His presence just went from the tip of my toes across my body. It was no mistaking that it was the Lord. He went straight out of the window behind me.

At that time, I jumped out of bed and began jumping and praising God. I danced, shouted, and praised. I don't know how long until I just fell backward on the bed from exhaustion. I did not have a single pain in my entire body. My arms were free, my legs and every part of my body rejoiced before the Lord. After I settled down and the weight of His presence lifted from the room, all but the fragrance remained. I just laid on the bed in total amazement of what had just happened. I have never felt that awesomeness of the Holy Spirit since that day. After what seemed like hours, I tried to get up and I could not move. I thought I was still intoxicated with the residue the presence of the Lord, so I waited a while to clear my head, and then I tried to get up.

Again, I could hardly move. I had no strength, but this was not the overwhelming presence I was feeling. This was something I recognized and had come to hate. It was a binding force, a painful disease, an unwanted attack that had bound me and paralyzed my body for almost two years. It had returned! I didn't understand, "What is this?" And that's when I asked, "Are you mocking me? What are you doing to me? "Why would You heal me and then take it away?" How was it possible to experience just a short while ago, the Lord in such an amazing, unexplainable, miraculous way, and now be bound in sickness, pain and seemingly defeat?

It was like a replay of just about two years ago: when I scooted backward up those steps and looked at that high bed with all those mattresses on it and how the children had to help me to get into bed.

I began to cry, and asked Him, "Lord, are you mocking me again? I told the Lord, I can't take this anymore." I could not believe it. I could not move. I closed my eyes and I began to pray for the Lord to take care of my children. I asked for two more personal things from Him to do for me. Then, I prayed for the Lord to take me home. I closed my eyes and waited for Him to come for me. After laying there on my daughter's bed for a long while. The Lord began to speak to me. The Father began to teach me about the finished work His Son had accomplished for me over Two Thousand years ago. Two Thousand years ago He took one of the stripes upon His back for arthritis. That day, my Savior suffered at Calvary for me. He finished His assignment, and that was for me. He arose the Victor.

The Lord spoke so kind and gentle, yet firm with authority. He said, “I didn't heal you today but, on that cross, I finished your healing so you wouldn't have to bear it. Delores, I healed you at Calvary.” I laid there while the Lord talked with me and I asked for forgiveness for wanting to die and I began to praise Him for life. This began the change in my life. This book cannot contain the pages of what God did for me those days as I learned to praise Him for HIs love to me.

I began to praise God with a new level of understanding and wisdom, new level of honor and love, and a new level of commitment and loyalty. I was beyond praising Him to receive or praising out of duty, but out of love for what He had done for me so long ago.

Praise will open up and reveal to you the root cause of sickness and disease. The Holy Spirit began teaching me on *generational curses* and how they affect the person and how to break the curse of arthritis which was in my bloodline.

I began to confess the sins and iniquities, of the forefathers, those I knew and those I did not know. I renounced and broke all sickness and disease passed down to me. I began to break through for my children and their children. I tapped into a realm of praise that took me into the Holy of Holies where I laid my life on the altar of sacrifice. Oh, the power in praise is so powerful. It is a fierce weapon against the enemy of your flesh.

I can't say how long after that it was nor can I give you a date my healing was manifested. All I know is because of the encounter I experienced with the Lord, change happened in my heart, and there was a gradual healing that began to be manifested.

The Lord led me through different levels of praise, and worship became a priority in my everyday life.

Today, I stand before you a woman who has been totally healed from rheumatoid arthritis, and for this, I give God all the glory.

Return to the Green House

Let him kiss me with the kisses of his mouth
for thy love is better than life.

Solomon 2:4

I must take you back to the green house to explain why this chapter is one of the most meaningful chapters of this book. Why go back to the green house? It was here where I truly found the source of my strength, the love of my life, and the beginning of my destiny.

It was here in this little house, that the book of Solomon opened up in my spirit, and I experienced a love so pure and precious such as I never thought possible on this earth

It was here, as the Holy Spirit led me to this particular book in the Holy Bible that I found my true love. It was here my life changed, and the love of Christ captured my soul.

It was in this place in my journey with God, that I understood with Christ that no mountain would be impossible to climb, no waters would be impossible to swim, and no battle would ever be able to defeat me.

Many may not understand this beautiful book of Solomon. It is a love story between Christ and His bride (church).

Several titles have been suggested for the book, all taken from the first verse: *The Song of Songs*, *The Song of Solomon*, or *Canticles*. The first title is a Hebrew way of expressing the superlative: *The Most Excellent Song*; the second denotes authorship; and the third means *Songs*, being taken from the Latin translation.

Let me first share, that I am in no way trying to interpret these verses in this book and say this is the interpretation for all. I just know personally what Christ revealed to me, changed my life and gave me joy and peace such as I never had.

In prayer, after work one beautiful evening, the children were asleep and I was in bed meditating and pondering over the Scriptures when the Holy Spirit led me to the book of Solomon. Opening the book, I began to read the verses, and there was absolutely no understanding of what I was reading. I put the Bible down beside me on the bed and I began to talk with the Lord asking what the meaning of the verse found in Solomon 2:4: "Let him kiss me with the kisses of his mouth for thy love is better than wine." I will reference the classic writer, the late, William Garnall.

God began to speak as to why the writer likened love to wine.

The Scriptural emphasis of wine is intended to be the symbol of the richest earthly joy. Man is not content with the drinking of wine as God originally intended it to be. The wine was at one time as common as bread on the table. As I speak on this verse, let's keep this in mind. I hope you will be able to embrace and experience the same revelation I received concerning Christ love for humanity.

Christ's Love Is Better Than Wine

There are different ideas and opinions connected with wine today. Some say, don't drink it, use it moderately, drink abundantly, but, there is no question concerning the Love of Christ. None of the Godly will say you've had too much, don't pray for more, it cost too much. No, God's love is without purchase. It is free. Why is this? Because, it seemed good in His sight. Christ's love is to be enjoyed without worrying about overindulging. The sweetest matter on earth if continually received will get tiring but, not the love of Christ. It will never change. It only gets sweeter and sweeter as the days go by. The poor drunkard gets sick from wine, but Healing comes from the wine of Christ. New Wine speaks of Joy and Praise

Christ's love is better than Wine because it is without flaw. It is imperfect; it must undergo a process before being considered perfect. As we look at all the joys of this earth, there is something which makes them imperfect, such as past relationships, friends and family and so on. Solomon lists all his works and what he did and had in Ecclesiastes 2:4-11.

"And whatever mine eyes desired I kept not from them. I withheld not my heart from any joy: for my heart rejoiced in all my labour: and this was my portion of all my labour.

Then I looked on all the works of my hands had wrought, and all the labour I had labored to do: and behold all was vanity and vexation of the spirit and there was no profit under the sun."

Anyone who delights in Christ's Love, will find it perfect, and pure because He is altogether lovely.

Charles Spurgeon wrote "All perfections melted into one perfection, and all beauties combined into one inconceivable beauty."

Christ Love Is Better than Wine...It Will Never Turn Sour

Husband and wives fall out of love today, and children come from loveless homes, but while we were yet sinners, Christ loved us so much He died on the Cross for us so we could live and experience His love.

Wine was often used as a medicine. It had healing aids in it. We can see this in the story of the Good Samaritan, who saw the man on the side of the road who had been robbed and beaten and left for dead. He ministered to him and poured oil and wine on his wounds. In Luke 10:33 Christ's love was poured out for us at Calvary for our healing for the spirit soul and body.

There are times it seemed as though the strength of the world was on my shoulders, bills, stress, work, the care of my children, and going to work when I felt I could hardly get out of the bed. This is when I would feel the oil and the wine of the Holy Spirit being poured over me, giving me the strength to keep on. The love of Christ would lift every weight, and I knew I could face the tomorrows.

Wine is also associated with Joy. Human joy is derived from earthly sources. True joy comes from New Wine (the Holy Ghost) there's no comparison.

Wives: If you would look at your husbands and say, "Honey I love you better than Wine." The response may be," yeah, thanks a lot, I love you too!"

Could it be that wine can be addictive? Intoxicating? Losing your natural senses? Control? We realize that there is a spiritual significance for Solomon to compare wine to love. The first miracle Jesus did was turning the water into wine, and it was at a wedding in Canaan. Some of you have never experienced True Love. There is a reason this writer likened Wine to Christ's Love

"Thus saith the Lord as the New Wine is found in the Cluster and one says destroy it not for a Blessing in it, so will I do for my servant's sakes, that I may not destroy them all" – Isaiah 65:8

God's Love in the Cluster.

Some of us have only experienced the love of Christ in the cluster form, not in the fullness of what He has for us.

The Wine is first in the cluster form of the grapes. Christ's love was stored up in old eternity. (Jesus was still with His Father).

Christ's love was still in the cluster not yet enjoyed. The Heavens were pregnant with the love of Christ not yet birthed. Many died in faith not tasting of the fullness of His love. It was not yet unveiled.

"Surely He has born our griefs and carried our sorrows yet we did esteem Him stricken and smitten of God, and afflicted." (Isaiah 53:4)

"But He was wounded for our transgression He was bruised for our iniquities, the chastisement or our peace was upon Him, and by His stripes, we are healed." (Isaiah 53:5)

Christ was still in the cluster form. Promises, prophesied from the prophets, but not yet fulfilled, The Unfailing Love of Christ was not yet unveiled.

The Love of Christ in The Basket

Remember, before the wine can be made it must be cast into the basket. The grapes are plucked from the vine and thrown in the basket for the next process of making the wine. Jesus left His ivory palaces and came down to earth. If He had not left Heaven, we never would have known His love in maturity.

The Sacred Vine was taken like the cluster of grapes and thrown in the basket of the earth in the womb of a woman. He stayed closed up in the womb prepared for Him until the appointed time. Our Savoir was then emptied out into the earth to begin His life.

We see the love of Christ as He walked the shores of Galilee healing the sick and raising the dead. We see His love as He had compassion for the woman at the well, and healed her empty life, giving her hope for a new day. We see His love in the temptation in the wilderness bearing the reproach and yet conquering for us.

"The spirit of the Lord is upon me because He hath anointed me to preach the gospel to the poor, he hath sent me to heal the brokenhearted to preach deliverance to the captive and recovering of the sight to the blind, to set liberty those that are bruised, to preach the acceptable year of the Lord." (Luke 4:18)

Christ' Love in the Winepress

It is the time for the crushing of the grapes. The grapes are now trampled on and the only thing left is the shell of the grape. In the garden, sweat like drops of blood ran down His face. He was smitten and spit upon His hair was plucked out, and He was nailed to the Cross of Calvary. He was obedient unto death even the Cross.

Through all the crushing of the grapes, you cannot taste the fullness of the wine. Nor do you have the fullness or the Unfailing Love of Christ at its fulfillment. The process is not over yet.

Can you see even now His love is sweeter than wine? Christ wanted us to know the depth of His love toward us.

Saying, “Father, if thou be willing, remove this cup from me: nevertheless, not my will, but thine, be done.” (Luke 22:42)

And when the sixth hour was come, there was darkness over the whole land until the ninth hour. At the ninth hour Jesus cried with a loud voice "My God My God why have you forsaken me." (Mark 15:33)

From The Winepress to the Flagon

“The love of His promises given to you

The love of His Providence for He rules for you

The love of His intercession, for He, pleads for you

The love of His representation for He sits on the right hand of His Father as a representative for His people" (Charles Spurgeon)

The wine must be stored after it is trampled on, and there poured into the flagon for its age. We see Jesus shut back up in Old Eternity WAITING!

Waiting for your praise, through the midst of your situations, trials, and frustrations. Waiting for the wine to mature so we would be able to know His unfailing, uncompromising, and sacrificial love toward us.

I do not know what you are going through, where you are in your walk with God; however, there is enough love from the Father to heal your pain. Your emotional trauma, your physical illness. Whatever you might need, love heals all.

Christ had to go through the pain and suffering, the trials and situations, Times of loneliness, but that was for us to know He did it all for us. He paved the way for us. His love is what will carry us through.

From the Flagon to the Cup

We would never know the fullness of the Father's love if it would have stayed in old Eternity, shut up in the womb of Heaven where we could not taste of it. Nor would those who drink the wine know the fullness of it if they only could taste the wine in the grape form.

It had to go through the process from the vine to the basket, from the basket to being trampled upon, then stored in the flagon. Jesus told them to wait in the Upper Room for the new wine of the Spirit to be poured out and on Pentecost.

“And suddenly, there came a sound from heaven as of a rushing mighty wind, and it filled all the house where they were sitting. And there appeared unto them cloven tongues like as of fire, and it sat upon each of them. And they were all filled with the Holy Ghost and began to speak with other tongues, as the Spirit gave them utterance. Others mocking said, these men are full of new wine." (Acts 2:2-3, 13)

Heaven opened its womb and poured out the love of Christ. They waited, praising God with open mouths. They did drink of the love of Christ in its fullness, and they were drunk.

"Taste and see that the Lord He is good" Christ has a Covenant Love for us. Before the Daystar knew its place, God loved us.

Jesus made a Covenant with God that He would bear our sins and suffer in our place. When we realize we are eternally chosen, eternally given to Christ, and eternally loved by Christ, then we will know His love is better than wine.

Christ has a Forbearing love for his church, the love that saw us fall into sin and the love that saw us speaking lies.

"He saw me ruined in the fall, yet loved me, notwith-standing all

He saved me from my lost estate, His loving-kindness, oh, how great."

"Awake, My Soul, to Joyful Lays" by Samuel Medley, 1738-1799

His promises are Yea and Amen! What He said He will do!

The Rose

I am the rose of Sharon, and the lily of the valleys.

Solomon 2:1

Hosea 2:14,15:

"Therefore, behold, I will allure her, and bring her into the wilderness, and speak comfortably unto her. And I will give her vineyards from thence, and the valley of Achor for a door of hope: and she shall sing there, as in the days of her youth, and as in the day when she came up out of the land of Egypt. And it shall be at that day, saith the LORD THAT thou shalt call me Ishi, and shalt call me no more Baali.

" It was in the little green house, that I truly fell in love with my Lord. It was there I heard the voice of my Beloved say to me "*You are my Rose!*"

Many would argue the interpretation that Christ is speaking about Himself here. All I know is that He spoke to me, and He confirmed it everywhere I went to minister. For over six years, I was given roses. I remember after ministering in Anchorage, Alaska. It was the closing night of the service and I had not received a rose, I remember asking God: "What happened? Where are you?" I had come to expect a rose from my love everywhere I went.

Finally, when it was time for me to walk up on the platform after the pastor had introduced me, he said, "Just a minute, I have to do this." He shared that the day before the Lord had spoken to him to buy me roses, so he told his wife to pick up a dozen yellow rose. She called him and said, "Why roses? Let me get her something she can keep." He said, "No, it must be roses and they must be yellow." He had the usher bring them and they presented them to me. I wept because the Lord had literally spoiled me and I was like a little child wondering what happened with our relationship. Did He forget? No, the Father can't forget.

At another meeting in Phoenix, Arizona, I was ministering in a revival. At the close of service, a little girl about ten years old was trying to get into the pastor's office to me. The assistant pastor was telling her, "No, you can't go in now Sister Kendrick is resting from ministering." I heard the child crying so I told him to let her in. She ran to me, and gave me the sweetest picture, she had drawn a picture of a rose.

I have had rings that were roses, bracelets, flowers, and yes pictures. When the Lord called me His rose, He said, "I will always give you roses as a reminder of the covenant I made with you many years ago." It was very personal, and He has allowed me to keep the covenant between the two of us. Why yellow? That, too, is a personal answer to a request made many years ago. However, the yellow rose stands also for joy and happiness, but most of all, yellow roses mean friendship. And the meaning of yellow roses is very special because it's associated with true friendship. A true friend is so important to people of all ages; it's like a gift from God.

"Many of the Jewish writers and some Christian interpreters take "I am the rose of Sharon...." to be the words of the church, expressing the excellency of her grace, loveliness, and beauty she had from Christ; and intimating also her being in the open fields, exposed to many dangers and enemies, and so needed his protection. The church may be compared to a "rose" for its beautiful color and sweet odor, and for its delight in sunny places, where it thrives best and is most fragrant.

This figure is exceeding just; not only the beauty of women is expressed by the color of the rose, as is common in poems of this kind; to give instances of it would be endless. No rose can be more beautiful in color, and delightful to the eye, than the church is in the eyes of Christ, as clothed with his righteousness, and adorned with the graces of His Spirit: nor is any rose of a more sweet and fragrant smell than the persons of believers are to God and Christ, being considered in him; and even their graces, when in exercise, yea, their duties, and services, when performed in faith; and, as the rose, they grow and thrive under the warming, comforting, and refreshing beams of the sun of righteousness, where they delight to be." (Gill's Exposition)

Yes, the little greenhouse, was a place of precious memories. It became my secret place, my place of refuge. It was there I first heard the audible voice of God. It was there visions were shared from the throne. It was there that I believe is what brought me to here, which is the key to my relationship with Christ.

Many are renewing their vows today. Some because it's just traditional. Others because they are trying to recapture that which has been lost.

Many marriages have grown cold. The honeymoon has long been over. The thrill and excitement that you once had for each other, is gone. The house is silent with the absence of communication. Legally married, just in the same house; however, the love which once filled the house with the fragrance of intimacy is gone.

Couples who once enjoyed and looked forward to those precious intimate moments are now going through the motions and duties of marriage, just satisfying the flesh.

Many times, it's no different with the Saints, They jump, shout, sing, they become emotional over the worship, or the message, (which is good) but, never experiencing the true joy of worship in their homes. Not until returning the next Sunday to church do they praise and enter into the joy of the Lord. We often live defeated lives through the week: heavy depression, thoughts of suicide, and the dreading facing another day. "What sense is it in getting up, there will be no different today than yesterday." So, you look for someone or something to fix you. (Something to give you a temporary fix.)

Listen, you can have affairs every day or one-night stands, but there is a place in Christ where you enter into a relationship, which is never-ending. It only gets sweeter as you grow in Him. It is in the secret place of the Highest. It takes a process of time to develop this kind of Relationship! No, I am not saying you do not have problems. You face disappointment and pain from time to time. But, when you have a relationship with Christ He is forever there to walk through them with you, He will never leave you, belittle you, abuse you, or make you feel unwanted.

It was during a time at the beginning of my relationship with the Father, that the mere sound of me saying HIS name sent chills all over me! The preacher of the book of Solomon says it this way: “His name is as ointment poured out.”- Solomon 1:3. Yes, God is a jealous God, "Kiss the Son lest He be angry with you." - Psalms 2:12

Because of the demands placed upon us in our daily schedule of business, our relationship with God becomes secondary. Prayer, Bible study, worship, and giving, all end up on the back burner so to speak.

As Israel failed to keep the passion burning hot for her God, even so, we allow our love to grow cold. We replace Him with the things of this world. There is nothing wrong with many of the things we must do, but when you place them before your commitment and service to the Father, they become an idol (TV. sports, jobs, alcohol, drugs, success, etc.).

Revelation 3:15, 16, Speaking to the church of Laodicea: "I know your deeds; you are neither cold nor hot. How I wish you were one or the other. So, because you are lukewarm — neither hot nor cold — I am about to spit you out of My mouth!"

Your Relationship with God will make you move from an experience in Him to a relationship with Him. This relationship will transform you into a new man or woman, boy or girl.

The love of God will give you a new love for your husband, wife, and children. Singles: this kind of love will take your eyes off of that guy or girl who is not for you and introduces you to the Real Lover so you will know what to look for in a mate.

It is like being in the outer court of the Tabernacle of Moses in Exodus 25. Draw me to the next level, I want to see your face. I want more. I have heard of your love but have not yet tasted of it to the fullness. I have been operating from my five senses of hearing, smelling, touching, tasting, and seeing, I have been on the outside gazing in through the latticework, and because of my pain, I have not been able to get to you.

"My beloved is like a roe or a young hart: behold, he standeth behind our wall, he looked forth at the windows, shewing himself through the lattice." (Solomon 2:9)

But the Father has removed all the latticework, all the veils so you can experience His Unfailing love. The Cry is draw me, Lord and we will run after thee.

We want to go beyond the Inner Court experience to the Holy of Holies. I do not want to stay in the outside of your court. The inner chambers are amazing, but I want MORE: pass the Brazen Altar, and beyond the place where I have to see something, touch, smell, hear or taste. No, I want to come through the inner courts. The Veil is gone. I can behold the glory of your love.

Some would say I have not experienced the Love of God. I have been so long in the desert, the wilderness, that I can't even feel His love anymore. Then let this be your song. Lord take me into the Holy of Holies. Take me to pass everything that would draw attention off you. Take me beyond seeing with the natural eye. Take me deeper until I come into you and our heart begin to beat as one.

The Love of God - His love will take you through the meanest battle. His love will heal a broken heart, His love will catapult you to the next level to the embracing of His arms, and the strength of His power.

The answer to intimacy with God is praise and worship. If you will practice praising God in all things, you will experience the victory over every obstacle that comes against you. Praise is a weapon because praise speaks of who God is and what He has done and what He will do. Praise will break through mountains and bring down strongholds. Praise will cause your enemy to bow before you. I'm talking about the enemy of sickness, disease, fear, rejection, lust, and unforgiveness. I could go on and on. Praise is the fourth son of Judah. He is a person. Let praise arise in your life. Live a life of praise, and you will see the mighty hand of God go before you, as it was in the armies of Israel. Your enemies will fall before you, and you will pick up the spoil.

Yes, it was in the greenhouse where I was planted in the soil of love. Deep in the soil of His word, I was cultivated and pruned for His glory. It was here I pledged to God my troth, my Lord and King. And in this place, I spoke my vows to my beloved. No longer have I called you master, (baali) but Ishi my husband my love.

"For your husband is your Maker--the LORD of Hosts is His name--the Holy One of Israel is your Redeemer; He is called the God of all the earth."
Isaiah 54:5

It was here my beloved called me ROSE!

My broken relationship produced

"A ROSE"

Your broken relationship doesn't have to

leave you broken.

Out of my broken relationship, I became whole.

Out of the ashes, came the diamond.

Out of the deep waters, came the pearl.

Out of the stony hills, came the gold.

Every young girl looks forward to the day when they will walk down that aisle with her prince. I was no different. Born in a family with my Father and mother very present in my life, I, too wanted the storybook wedding and the *till death do us part* marriage.

I met my husband in high school, fell in love and later married with great expectation of being the best wife in the world. As I walked down the aisle, my mind was racing with all these questions: Are you making a mistake? Are you sure? Maybe you should stop and run like Julie Roberts did in 'Runaway Bride'. It's not too late. I guess all brides have some questions as they walk down that long aisle. I was no different.

After settling into marriage for a while, it was sweet. I loved cooking and preparing meals. Enjoyed the whole routine of marriage, but after a while, things began to change. My marriage relationship became abusive, verbally, physically and emotionally, not long after marriage.

What makes a woman stay in an abusive relationship? Some say they do not want to be alone, while others are too fearful to leave because their lives have been threatened, some have become codependent, and others say because of religious beliefs. I was just in love and thought my love coupled with prayer was strong enough to birth change.

My prayer is that you will be encouraged and inspired as you read my story. If you are in an abusive relationship you will have the courage to get out while you can. No, it wasn't supposed to be like this. I was an innocent young lady. I guess you could say naïve and ignorant about life. I had four brothers older than I growing up. But I never was out there doing my thing. However, it didn't take long for me to become educated about life.

My mother raised me with the principle that: girls don't do everything that the guys do. So, I settled into my routine of marriage. Over the years, we had two beautiful daughters and rather than things getting better, they became worse.

Now, as I share with you, I want you to understand that it takes two to make a marriage work, so I am not placing blame. However, I want you to know that when marriage becomes abusive, there is no book that says you should remain in it and be stripped of your identity as a person.

My marriage became very abusive; first, verbal abuse and of course as we know it never stops there. It will eventually escalate to physical abuse. This time is critical, as decisions you make *now* is very important. Are you going to stay in it or are you going to get out?

About the Author

Apostle Delores L. Kendrick is the Founder of Tabernacle of Praise Church located in Seattle, Washington. Apostle Kendrick has served in ministry for over 40 years. She has been called for this season to equip the saints, according to Ephesians chapter four, in higher dimensions of spiritual warfare, which will prepare them for Kingdom living and Kingdom Service. Her prophetic voice is known nationally, as well as, internationally.

God has given Apostle Kendrick a love and burden for the nations. In 2007, Kendrick Ministries was established as an outreach for equipping the body of Christ for the in-time ministry. Her passion is to see leaders in the five-fold ministry serve in a spirit of excellence.

Apostle Kendrick's first book, *Women of Excellence*, is also available at Amazon.com, Barnes and Noble.